And Then
I Had Kids

And Then I Had Kids

Encouragement for Mothers of Young Children

Susan Alexander Yates

WORD PUBLISHING

Word (UK) Ltd
Milton Keynes, England

WORD AUSTRALIA
Kilsyth, Victoria, Australia

WORD COMMUNICATIONS LTD
Vancouver, B.C., Canada

STRUIK CHRISTIAN BOOKS (PTY) LTD
Maitland, South Africa

ALBY COMMERCIAL ENTERPRISES PTE LTD
Balmoral Road, Singapore

CHRISTIAN MARKETING NEW ZEALAND LTD
Havelock North, New Zealand

JENSCO LTD
Hong Kong

SALVATION BOOK CENTRE
Malaysia

AND THEN I HAD KIDS

Copyright © 1988 by Susan Alexander Yates.

First published in the USA by Wolgemuth & Hyatt, Brentwood, Tennessee.

First UK edition Word (UK) Milton Keynes, England 1992.

ISBN 0–85009–557–3   (Australia ISBN 1–86258–202–5)

Reproduced, printed and bound in Great Britain for Word (UK) Ltd. by Cox & Wyman Ltd., Reading.

92 93 94 95 / 10 9 8 7 6 5 4 3 2 1

With love and thanksgiving
to my husband, Johnny,
and our children,
Allison, John, Christopher,
Susy, and Libby

CONTENTS

FOREWORD

This is a book that is entertaining, human, and helpful.

It is well-written and relevant—a book that parents of young children (and grandparents!) can identify with and be encouraged by.

Susan Yates writes: "Seeing life in seasons enables us to get some perspective in our lives. In every season there will be trials and joys. Hardly anything lasts forever. We need to see our life in seasons and rejoice in the season at hand. As we relax and begin to soak up the unique blessings of this particular season, we will begin to experience and to enjoy the incredible richness of life." I found that I had a new awareness of these seasons as well as a desire to savor them to the fullest after reading Susan's book.

One of the aspects of being a Christian family is being ready to serve each other. My oldest son, Daniel, was impressed when the Yates' twins offered to wash the great piles of dishes after a meal with Daniel and his family in Austria. "They had such a good time doing it for us all," he said, "that their joy of service was contagious." When I heard this, I thought of Susan's words, "When our home is full of little people, we have a captive audience that is readily molded into a growing Christian family."

May this book be used to create homes "with an atmosphere of love, forgiveness, and laughter," which in turn will bring healing to a broken world.

—Ingrid Trobisch
Author

ACKNOWLEDGMENTS

Many people have helped make this book a reality. In essence, this is a family story. The support and encouragement of my husband, Johnny, and my children, Allison, John, Christopher, Susy, and Libby made the whole project possible.

The people of The Falls Church (Episcopal) and my Tuesday morning prayer group prayed for me and willingly shared their stories with me.

My parents, Fran and Syd Alexander, gave me a solid foundation and preparation for which I am humbly grateful. The families of my sister and brothers—Fran and Catlin Cade, Syd and Laurie Alexander, Frank and Joan Alexander—offered their encouragement as well. A bonus in my life has been the tremendous influence of my mother-in-law, Sue Tucker Yates.

Weekly, I benefited from the professional advice and deep personal friendships of Ann Hibbard and Beth Spring. Ann Holladay, Gail Hyatt, and Julie Henderson also encouraged me in many ways.

For the past twenty years, Chuck and Cathy Miller have influenced our lives. Many of the thoughts on priorities, real needs, felt needs, and areas of growth come from their teaching.

I am also grateful to my publishers, Robert Wolgemuth and Michael Hyatt, and to my editor, George Grant, who believed in me and demanded the best. Their company itself is a "family" of which I am happy to be a part.

INTRODUCTION

Dashing down the steps to do yet another load of wash, I realized that something was not quite right. At first it was merely a subconscious feeling of discomfort. As I sorted the clothes for washing, my uneasiness increased. What was wrong?

Suddenly I realized the problem. The house was *too* quiet. Silence had replaced the normal loud noise level, and silence meant trouble where toddlers were concerned. What were my eighteen-month-old twins into now?

Quickly I began the search. My three older children had not seen the girls. I frantically looked in each room, calling, "Susy! Libby! Where are you?"

Only silence answered back.

Then I saw the evidence—little black footprints running across the brand new carpet in the family room. The fireplace was a mess with ashes spilling out onto the floor. I followed the footprints into the utility room where they came to an abrupt halt in front of the freezer.

Packages of frozen food had spilled out across the floor as if an avalanche had tumbled from my freezer. The freezer door was ajar, and from within I could hear squeals of delight and a language of nonsense as toddlers entertained each other. Peering inside, I found two little girls black with soot joyfully looking at books!

Our children came into the world with great energy and many demands. By the time they had all arrived, Allison, our oldest daughter, had just turned seven; John was four; Christopher, two; and the twins, Susy and Libby, were brand new babies. With a bang I had joined the ranks of the "overwhelmed mother."

Our twins were a big surprise. We found out there would be two instead of one just three weeks before they were born. Six weeks after Susy and Libby arrived, we moved to a new state. We had no family nearby. The twins were colicky and did not sleep. I had no help, and I did not know anyone. My husband was in a demanding new job with only a tiny support staff.

For the first several months we lived in our new home, our kitchen was gutted for a renovation. I remember doing dishes in the bathroom sink and eating cold cuts because the stove was on the porch. When the kitchen was finally finished, a severe storm hit causing a tree to crash into it. Construction had to begin all over again!

Since I was nursing the colicky twins, those early days required a monumental effort in order for me to make it until nap time. I often felt that my brain had stopped working. Twice in one week I went grocery shopping and arrived home only to realize that I had forgotten to bring the groceries home from the store!

All in all, my expectations of family life before I had kids were indeed different from the reality that I faced with five children. I used to be critical of moms whose children had runny noses. "Why don't their mothers wipe their faces?" I would wonder in amazement. I would marvel at a child in public whose hair looked like it had not been brushed in a week or whose clothes did not match. And then I had kids!

There went my six-year-old son off to school in a striped shirt and checkered pants (not the style of the day). My eight-year-old daughter had long beautiful hair to the middle of her back. But it looked like a rat's nest that particular morning. Once I lost track of the twins (aged two) right before an important ballgame for another one of my children. I found them hiding in their closet with Desitin ointment, happily covering each other's hair and bodies with the sticky white goo. We had no time to clean properly, so off we went to the ballgame and the curious glances of all those parents who had "clean" kids.

Living with five young children has indeed been a challenge. It has also been tremendously enlightening. As I have contemplated my own situation and talked with other mothers who have also been dealing with small children, it has become evident that there are specific problems we all have in common.

Chapter 1 is a quick overview of those common challenges. There I will raise many questions. But don't give up! The answers follow.

Chapters 2 through 9 look at each of the challenges in some detail, then outline ways those challenges can be met and even overcome.

And finally, in Chapter 10, we will explore ways that those challenges can actually evolve into principles for family living that will be relevant for us throughout the rest of our lives.

This book is designed to be used for personal encouragement. It can also effectively be used in small groups for study and discussion. My prayer is that as you read it, you will be comforted by understanding, refreshed with laughter, and stimulated with ideas to enable your time as a young mother to be one of unique and lasting joy.

THE HASSLED MOTHER

Early one morning a repairman arrived in the middle of breakfast to fix our broken stove. As he worked close by, the choruses of tiny voices and spoons banging on high chairs got louder and louder.

"But I don't like any of them!" wailed my three-year-old as he studied the seven different boxes of cereal on the breakfast table.

"The red one is yuck," came the authoritative opinion of his five-year-old brother.

"Why can't we have pancakes?" pleaded seven-year-old Allison.

A loud crash interrupted my response as a cup landed on the floor sending little rivers of milk running around dropped Cheerios.

"Oh," I groaned as I frantically searched for some towels to block the spill from reaching the repairman's toolbox.

Susy and Libby, my year-old twins, had already covered the floor and themselves with more breakfast than they had eaten. Their small bodies were sticky messes—I even noticed a few Cheerios implanted in their hair. As I crawled under the table to wipe up the spilled milk, the repairman watched in amazement.

"Mrs. Yates," he finally said, "it must be awfully *hard* to raise all these children."

I'm sure that our breakfast was to him an overwhelming catastrophe. To me it was *normal* chaos.

Actually, at that stage of my life, I was too tired to think that what I was doing was *hard*. I knew it was a challenge; I knew it was exhausting; and I knew it was often frustrating and without instant satisfaction.

Several times I found myself wondering if other mothers were experiencing the same feelings and frustrations that I was. Often a frustration is not recognized until someone else verbalizes it, and we find ourselves saying, "Why, that's just how I feel!" There is great comfort and encouragement in realizing that you are not the only one who feels like this.

All too often though we're so swamped with the day-to-day necessities of mothering that we never actually have a chance to talk about our challenges and frustrations with others. We may even feel embarrassed because our problems seem so mundane in a world full of major crises. The fact is, though, a general feeling of depression is much better handled when we can put a name to our problems and examine their causes. Then we can look for creative solutions.

As I've lived at the center of a chaotic household overrun by small children, I've been greatly relieved to discover that several of the challenges I have had to face are actually *common* to most young mothers.

When we briefly identify eight of our most common problems, we will be encouraged in knowing that there are many women who are experiencing the same feelings that we are. In focusing on each of these challenges in detail, we will be inspired as we understand God's perspective on our situations. Finally, we will be refreshed as we discover many practical solutions. In this process, our challenges will evolve into principles that will enable us not only to endure but also to enjoy this special time as mothers of young children.

Low Self-Image

Late one summer afternoon, my husband, Johnny, arrived home from work to find me in a state of excitement. As I stood dripping with sweat, a big grin spread over my face when I exclaimed, "Hi, honey, I mowed the lawn for you." An astonished but pleased look crossed Johnny's face.

"What got into you?" he asked.

I replied, "I'm not sure, but I know I feel good because I have finally done something that lasts more than two days."

It is often difficult for moms with young children to accomplish anything that seems to last longer than a few hours. In a house with five small children, I found that clean kids were dirty quickly, a neat house lasted only through naptime, and dinner was a far cry from a gourmet meal. Mowing the lawn gave me a real sense of satisfaction—it lasted a few days!

In a world where material success and progress have become indicators of self-worth, it is very difficult for mothers to have anything of value to point to at the end of each day. There doesn't seem to have been major "progress" on anything important. Somehow bathing and dressing children don't qualify as "important" in the way we see things. We have not achieved any measurable "success." The children still fuss at nap time; they still spill everything; they continue to fight and even to bite.

If we have left a career to stay home with children, this may be even harder because we are accustomed to affirmation and recognition by the world. It is highly unlikely that your five-year-old will walk up to you and say, "Boy, Mom, you are doing a great job of raising me."

Reading *Green Eggs and Ham* by Dr. Seuss, for the fourth time, putting on tennis shoes again, or cleaning up the kitchen only to have it dirty five minutes later is more likely to produce frustration than fulfillment. In addition, the sheer exhaustion of caring for small children seems to have dulled our brains and sapped our creative energy.

Getting up to nurse babies night after night produces a continual sense of fatigue. Often the day seems like an endurance race—we just want to get through it. If we just had something to show for this fatigue, it might make a difference. But we don't. And so we don't feel very valuable to anyone. We simply feel tired, and our self-image sinks.

Well, if I can be a good mother to these children and have a happy loving home, it will all be worth it, we tell ourselves. Then we punish a child who was not at fault. Our self-image slips another notch. We can't even succeed one day at mothering without failing.

We tell ourselves that what we are doing is important. These are our children, and we are investing valuable time in raising them. We know we love them and we want to spend time with them, yet often we don't enjoy it at all. Then we feel guilty because we *should* be enjoying it, we think. We feel that what we are doing is right, and yet sometimes we don't like it. These feelings of guilt lower our self-image even more.

The world around us whispers that material progress and success are the criteria for self-worth. But mothers with small children do not experience instant progress or success. Are we thus doomed to a low self-image?

What should our self-worth really be based on? Is it possible, during the normal stresses of coping with small children, to maintain a positive self-worth? How can we do it? How can we, in recognizing our common problems, turn them into positive building blocks for a healthy self-image? What are practical things that we can do to feel better about ourselves and to know that we are valuable?

Stuck in a Rut

I groaned as I heard the small cries coming from the twins' room. The blackness of the night still wrapped its arms around the house. Surely it couldn't be morning already. Through one half-opened eye, I glanced at the flourescent clock. It was already 5:30 a.m. "Oh no!" I moaned and put the pillow on top of my head to block out the increasing wails of two hungry babies.

I'm not sure I can face another day, I sighed. Another day of nursing babies, feeding children, building block castles, cleaning house, doing laundry, and longing for the day to be over. The monotony of it all seemed overwhelming. I felt "stuck in a rut" with no end in sight.

It is easy for mothers of young children to find themselves suffering from monotony. There appears to be no end in sight to our daily tasks. We get through one day, go to bed, and awaken the next morning to find the very same chores facing us again.

A sense of isolation surrounds us, and we feel alone in our tasks. Much of our day is spent by ourselves entertaining and caring for small children. The absence of other adult conversation can cause us to feel like our brains have turned to mush. In addition, we may be ashamed of our feelings of frustration. Perhaps we hesitate to share our emotions with a friend because we are embarrassed. And that loneliness then compounds the feeling of being stuck in a rut. We are fearful that we won't be understood and accepted.

Because our hands are full with seemingly simple tasks, we may find that small issues upset us more than we feel they should.

The living room that was clean this morning is already a mess by lunch time, and we are irritated. Why do the children have to mess up every room? One of our toddler's shoes is missing again right when we need to go to the grocery store. Who ever thought shoes could become such a source of irritation?

Somehow the pictures we had of family life did not include runny noses, upset tummies, messy homes, whining children, and exhausted moms. We had envisioned clean babies happily cooing at their parents. Our anticipation had been one of total fulfillment once we had kids. Is it any wonder that our experience is tinged with disillusionment?

Is it possible to sense fulfillment in a household of small children? How do we acquire a proper perspective on this special time in our lives? Is it possible for this season to become one of enjoyment rather than of pure endurance?

Too Many Demands

The church nursery was overflowing as I arrived one Sunday morning for our worship service. I eagerly looked forward to Sunday mornings because I knew the children would be well cared for in their classes. At last I would have one peaceful hour to worship. However, today the situation in the nursery was desperate. There were simply too many two-year-olds and not enough adults. Could I please stay and help out?

With a weak smile of agreement, I plopped my purse on the shelf and raced to separate two toddlers who were playing "tug of war" with a picture book. At least, I thought, after a morning of twelve two-year-olds, my house of five children should be a piece of cake. As I helped other mothers care for the children that morning, we found ourselves discussing the need for more volunteers to assist in the Sunday School program.

There were also needs in the school system, needs in the neighborhoods, and needs in my husband's work. The numerous demands of my children alone could keep me occupied all day. Everywhere I looked someone seemed to need me.

The challenge of overwhelming demands faces all mothers. Mothers with young children are especially affected by numerous requests for help. If we do not work outside the home, the assumption is that we are readily available and have plenty of time to donate. Because so many women have begun to combine professional careers with child raising, the volunteer force has been depleted. Thus, there is a greater demand for those who are at home to fill the void. A mother at home can easily be overwhelmed by the many requests for her time and energy.

Women who do work outside the home in addition to raising children will also find themselves pressured by various nagging needs. *How can I*, she asks herself, *do an adequate job at the office and still give my children what they need?* The stresses upon her are almost too great as she attempts to do a good job in two worlds.

It is easy for us as busy mothers to find ourselves pulled in too many directions. Our husbands need us, our children need us, and our community needs us. The needs are valid and we would like to help, but there does not seem to be a way to fit it all in. In addition to all that outside pressure, we feel we will suffocate if we do not have time for ourselves.

Often we lack a clear purpose for our lives. Perhaps we find ourselves responding to each request without a sense of direction. The needs and the demands are great, yet how do we discern what is right for us? Is it possible to be the mother and wife I desire and still have time for myself? There are so many voices telling us how to live that we have to wonder who is right. How do we discern what our priorities should be? Does the Bible offer us any guidance in determining priorities? Are there really priorities that will work in any situation?

Not Enough Time with My Husband

Sitting on the park bench, I watched my boys kick the soccer ball back and forth across the grassy field. The twins were collecting rocks nearby to feed their "babies" along with a mixture of leaves and sticks.

Close by, on another bench, sat a couple who were deeply involved in an animated conversation. Delighted laughter punctuated their discussion. They seemed to be unaware of anyone else, so focused was their attention on each other. Every now and then he would give her an affectionate hug. I noticed they both wore wedding rings. They must be newlyweds, I mused with a pang of jealousy and wisdom. Just wait until they have kids!

Children bring great joy to a couple. They also bring an end to the honeymoon.

No longer is there as much freedom in schedules to spend time together. Demands upon both partners increase as the family grows. The years when we have young children are likely to be years of stress from many areas. Perhaps it's a crucial time in our husbands' career. Most likely our own careers have been affected by children. A move might be in the plans. Financial concerns may be on our minds. In the complexity of life, we may realize that we do not seem to have time to spend with our husbands, or that if we do spend time together, we do not enjoy it very much. We look longingly at a couple "in love" and wish for that carefree affection to return.

The expectations that we had of marriage may not have been met. What happened to the romantic man we fell in love with? Romance does not seem so important to him anymore. Intimate conversation may have fallen by the wayside. Our communication may have resorted to the functional. Who is paying the bills? What shall we do for vacation? Who will attend the civic meeting?

We may feel that our husbands are not meeting our needs, or that they are not sympathetic to the challenges we face with small children. Possibly we resent his career which takes him away from the family. There may be a sore subject in our relationship that we are afraid to discuss. It is too difficult and often causes dissension.

We are both stretched in so many ways. We are exhausted by children, and he's exhausted by the demands of a career. We do not appear to have the time or the energy to put into our own relationship. We know our marriage is important, yet it is often put aside in light of what seem to be more urgent demands. We long to restore the sense of fun and pure joy we used to have in being together. How can we make time for ourselves when we have young children?

Is it possible to work on a marriage when we are both so busy? How can we grow as best friends in the midst of so many demands? During these crucial years in our marriage, what can we do to ensure that we develop habits that will encourage a joyful marriage that will last for many years to come?

What Discipline Philosophy?

At last, I thought with great hope, *I believe the twins are potty trained.* My hope seemed well founded—for two days. One morning Libby appeared with a painful expression on her face. "What's the matter, honey?" I asked her.

"Nuttin', Mommie," she replied.

Nevertheless, her obvious wiggles and now awkward walk immediately gave away her problem.

"Libby," I asked, "did you wet your panties?"

"No, Mommie," came the reply. "Susy did it!"

This particular incident caused me to dissolve in laughter; however, the implications were typical of the challenges facing me in my effort to discipline my children. It was normal for my two-year-old to lie and to try to blame her sister. Nevertheless, these were tendencies that I knew my husband and I would have to change if we were to raise our children to be adults with integrity and personal responsibility.

Often we observe things in our children that we instinctively know should not be allowed. However, sometimes we do not understand the best way to bring about change. This is not a surprising dilemma. Conflicting advice is offered by many experts today on matters of discipline. Even among Christians there is sometimes disagreement on the most effective means of training our children.

With a variety of philosophies on discipline, our self-confidence in our own ability can become shaken. Perhaps we were raised with an approach vastly different from our husbands', and thus we have found that we disagree on matters of discipline. As a result, we constantly contradict each other and confusion follows.

How firm should our discipline be? Will I damage my child's spirit? How can I communicate love and discipline at the same time? What is acceptable at what age? How do I determine reasonable consequences for behavior?

Small children are incredibly creative in the trouble they discover. A neighbor once found my twins climbing into a manhole in the driveway. Somehow the heavy lid had been removed. Obviously, this was quite dangerous, and I asked my girls, "Didn't you know that this was dangerous?"

"You never told us, Mommie," was the response.

"I can't think of everything you might try," I exclaimed.

In our efforts to train our children, we may recognize that we do not have a clear philosophy of discipline. We lack a sense of direction and defined goals for our training. Are there Biblical guidelines for training in discipline? How can I formulate a practical plan that my husband and I can agree on? Frequently, I feel like my children are in charge. Is it possible for me to be in control in this household of strong-willed children? Can discipline training be a positive experience?

An Atmosphere of Tension

As a youngster, I remember going to visit a new friend whom I'll call Laura. Laura was very popular in school, and I was delighted to have been invited to her home. I hoped that she would like me. As I walked up the drive to her house, I was a bit nervous about my visit. What would her family be like and what would we do? I rang the doorbell and after a long wait, her mother appeared.

"Oh, it's you," she said in a bored manner.

Fortunately, Laura arrived and off we went to play. Throughout the afternoon her mother fussed at the children, screamed at the dog, and complained about her work. Generally, we did our best to stay out of her way. When I arrived home, my mother asked, "Susan, did you have fun at Laura's?"

"It was okay," I replied, "but next time I'd rather have her here."

At that point in my life, I would not have been able to define the depressed feeling in Laura's home. Today I recognize it as an atmosphere of tension. Laura's mother was probably not even aware of the negative atmosphere that dominated her home. If she was, she seemed powerless to change it.

We, too, may not be aware of the atmosphere in our homes. Certainly we want an atmosphere that radiates a positive, inviting, happy spirit. The atmosphere in our home is created either by default or by design. As busy mothers, it is easy to fall into the habit of nagging and complaining. Perhaps we take our task so seriously that we fail to laugh at ourselves. We may experience guilt or failure, and then depression results because we forget about forgiveness. Appreciation and acceptance may be lacking. In addition, the roles of service and sacrifice may have gotten lost in the shuffle. Praise and thanksgiving may have become the rarest of ingredients.

We desire to have a home marked by love, forgiveness, and joy. We want to experience these traits in our own lives. How can we allow God's supernatural love for us to shape the atmosphere in our homes?

Of course, each of our families is different with unique gifts and interests. Our family should not look exactly like anyone else's. Knowing that, how can we best encourage our family's talents in shaping the atmosphere of our home?

The most obvious components in homes full of small children often are confusion and chaos. Little can change that. But that confusion can be happy or it can resemble a battlefield. What ingredients make the difference in our homes? Is it possible to develop a practical plan that will enable us to create an atmosphere of joy?

Help and Support for Parents

I slipped in the front door from a date with my high school boyfriend. Weary from a busy day of work and caring for four children, my parents were already asleep. Gently I shook Mom and whispered, "I'm home, Mom."

"Did you have fun?" she asked in a sleepy voice.

"Yes."

"Good night, Sweetie. Please lock the front door."

I locked the front door and walked out the back door. Mary Turner's light was still on next door. A close friend of my parents, Mary Turner was a widow with a daughter my age. She was usually up late at night and many times I would go and visit with her after I returned home. Over cookies and punch, she'd hear about my date and listen with interest to whatever was on my mind. She asked me hard questions, gave me advice, and was available to me. Her values were the same as those of my parents, and by her willingness to spend time with me she offered support to my parents. In essence, she was an adult model in my life whose influence had a positive impact.

Parenting can be a lonely occupation. When we look around for people to emulate and for our children to follow, we are often disappointed. With family frequently living far away, we do not have a built-in support system that earlier generations did. The high divorce rate has left us with fewer models of two-parent families to whom we can go for encouragement. The increasing influence of the media has propelled into prominence celebrities that we do not always admire.

We need to have good role models in our lives to whom we can go for guidance as we raise our children. So often we long to ask the advice of someone who has already been through what we are experiencing. Did they ever have a similar problem with their child? How did they handle it? We need older adults who will not only encourage us in parenting but also help us grow in our faith.

We want to provide role models for our children as well. We need other adults who will befriend our children and to whom our kids will go for advice. Is it possible to find role models for ourselves and for our children in today's world? How can we train our children in discernment so that they know whom to follow and whom to avoid? What creative steps can we take to be role models for other people?

A Boring or Exciting Christian Home

The family was gathered around the dinner table. It was chilly outdoors and the Christmas tree lights glowed in the background. The three young children were full of excitement as they discussed the coming of Christmas.

"I wonder what I will get? I want a truck!"

"A doll is better than a truck."

Enthusiasm and anticipation radiated through the faces of the small children as their excitement grew. Dad began to tell the children the story of Jesus' birth and the true meaning of Christmas. In simple terms he struggled to explain how God became man and was born in a manger. His story and explanations seemed well received by his three young children. Suddenly the youngest boy looked up and, with child-like seriousness asked, "Daddy, who borned God?"

Young children are very receptive to spiritual truths; they are inquisitive and they believe easily. During these early years we have a unique opportunity to begin to teach them about God. This is a privilege. It is also a responsibility that we often do not know how to fulfill.

In considering the most effective way to have a Christian family, we often find that we have more questions than we do answers. We know we should teach our children about God, yet we are unsure how to do it. We may fear that we will not be able to answer their questions adequately. After all, there is much that we ourselves do not understand. In addition, when we look at our own lives, we know that we do not live as we should. We wonder if it is hypocrisy to try to teach our children how to live when we ourselves often fail.

We want our instruction to be exciting, but, alas, the children groan when we reach for our Bibles and a feeling of "necessary boredom" settles over the table. "Do we have to read today, Mom?" can be a typical response.

Prayer times offer a challenge as well. Our children may refuse to pray, or they may pray silly prayers. We wonder how we should respond. Perhaps we want to pray specifically, yet we find ourselves hesitant, because if God does not seem to answer, we fear our child will not believe.

Perhaps our concern is that we will pressure our children too much. After all, should we want them to be able to decide for themselves what to believe? In our confusion, it is easy to leave the Christian training of our children to the Church. However, whereas the Church can help, its main role is to be supportive of what takes place in the home. We have the most time with our children, and the Christian faith is not meant for Sundays alone, but for every day.

Young children are at their most receptive age; our challenge is clear. How can we build a creative Christian home? Is it possible to have prayer become a natural occurrence in our homes? Can the Bible become relevant not only for our children but for us as well? How can we take advantage of fellowship for our families? We want our homes to be places where each family member is growing in Christ. How do we help this happen in a way that is not awkward or forced but natural and exciting?

Principles That Last

Several moms were sitting around a swimming pool watching their children splash with delight. More water was coming out of the toddler area than was left in the pool. In between "emergency rescue" missions, the mothers chatted about the challenges of raising small children. Their empathy for one another served as an encouragement.

"Surely this time in our lives has to be the most difficult," remarked one young mother as she looked longingly over toward the adult pool where older mothers calmly swam laps.

In a few minutes her friend with teenagers came over from the adult pool to visit the moms and their small children. After listening to them discuss their sleepless nights, long days, and difficulties in discipline, she remarked, "Just wait. You think you have it hard now. It only gets worse."

During the next several minutes she described life with teenage children, painting a picture of doom and gloom. Sadly, this is too often the case when a mother with small children talks to a mother of adolescents.

Sometimes a mother of teens does struggle and agonize to a greater degree than do her younger friends. However, all-in-all, the season of older children can be one of greater enjoyment. Especially when early challenges were met with timeless solutions—solutions that together form a philosophy of parenting and of life that works throughout our lives.

The challenges that mothers of young children face are not unique. Each one has been experienced by someone else somewhere else. Across the ocean there is a mother struggling with her self-image. In a big city another mother doubts her ability to discipline effectively. In a different culture across the continent, a mother seeks ways to help her children grow in their faith. On a small farm a couple attempts to strengthen their marriage while caring for several little children.

There are solutions to each one of those dilemmas. And they are solutions that can make a difference in our lives for the rest of our lives.

As we explore in detail the universal challenges mothers face in the next few chapters, we will discover those philosophical principles that will indeed enable us to implement creative, practical solutions. In the process not only will we be encouraged in our family life now, we will also gain confident assurance for the joyful years to come as well.

Focus Questions

Meditate on Isaiah 40:10-11 and John 10:14-16.

1. What images describe the character of Christ? How might I be like a sheep?
2. List the most prominent challenges in my life right now.

Meditate on Psalm 28:6-9 and Jeremiah 29:11-13. What promises do I see here for me?

T W O

MAINTAINING A POSITIVE SELF-IMAGE

With my coat already on and my purse in hand, I pressed my nose against the cold windowpane looking for the headlights of my husband's car. The blackness of an early winter night wrapped itself around the house enhancing my feelings of claustrophobia.

I clenched my teeth and shut my ears to the two-year-old twins' whining voices coming from the top of the stairs. *It's another earache, I'm sure*, I reflected with a feeling of resignation. In another corner of the house I could hear my eight-year-old and my six-year-old fighting over a board game. My four-year-old was again crying at my side as he had just bumped himself for what seemed like the tenth time that day. I patted his head more out of habit than compassion.

Unhappy choruses came shouting at me from every corner of the house. I tightened my fists and thought, *I've got to escape*. There was still laundry to be done, toys to be picked up and supper dishes to be cleared away. *Why, I haven't accomplished anything today*, I felt as I looked out into the night, longing for the car to turn into the driveway.

Finally the two lights appeared. Before he was even halfway up the walk, I dashed out the front door to meet my husband. "I love you, Johnny," I said, "but I'm leaving. You've heard of runaway children. Well, I'm a runaway parent. I'll be back in a little while, but they're all yours for now—and they're all screaming."

Ah, what bliss to walk in complete solitude around a shopping mall with hundreds of other Christmas shoppers and no one who needs me or talks to me or wants me right this minute! As I reflected on my exhausted state and my need to "run away," I wondered if there were any other discouraged mothers in this milling crowd of shoppers. Surely there were other mothers who were also experiencing burnout. I was discouraged, frustrated, and physically exhausted. I felt I had lost control of the seemingly simple tasks of running a household.

Before our children were born, I'd been able to cope with an important job, run a home, and be a reasonably good wife with a real sense of satisfaction and accomplishment. I naturally assumed I would be just as effective in parenting. I had come from a wonderful, loving home, had a great husband whose values matched mine, and had been exposed to a lot of good books and lectures on building a Christian family.

None of this, however, had prepared me for the biggest challenge I found myself facing in parenting small children: a plummeting view of my own self-worth. As I walked in temporary peace around the shops aglow with Christmas lights, I reflected on this phenomenon of low self-esteem that young mothers often experience, the sense of isolation that a mom feels as she copes with the endless tasks of mothering.

Sometimes it's embarrassing to share with another friend this sense of depression because it seems so silly. After all, we're bright, highly motivated people. We should be able to handle these small children with ease, we think. So we keep these feelings to ourselves while our image and self-worth crumble.

We need to realize that all mothers surrounded by small children experience many common struggles. Whether we work at home or pursue a part-time or full-time profession in addition to being mom, we all share many of the same problems and challenges. Honestly admitting the battle of maintaining a positive self-image will go a long way toward helping to find solutions to this common problem. As I've experienced this in my own life and talked to other young mothers, there seems to be some consensus on the specific causes of low self-worth. It's helpful to explore these causes, to see what God would say to us in our situation, and to develop some creative solutions for dealing with this common problem.

Frustration, fatigue, guilt, and failure are four agents that will combine to plague every young mother with feelings of a negative self-worth.

Frustration

Frustration is one of the most common struggles for moms who are surrounded by small children. There are a variety of reasons. A friend with several small children recently shared with me that her frustration came in part because she felt a loss of control. Her children had been sick for two weeks, and nothing she had planned had turned out the way she expected. When our twins were small, they had continual ear infections. I saw our pediatrician more than I did my husband. One night I actually dreamed about him and woke my husband up in a panic.

Frustration is also caused by monotony. Every day is likely to be the same, and there appears to be no end in sight to runny noses, dirty diapers, and cereal all over the floor! Days run into weeks. Weeks run into months. Life begins to blur into one long mind-numbing series of chores.

Lack of accomplishment is another source of frustration. With small children, it's difficult to do anything that lasts. That's why I enjoyed mowing the lawn. It lasted a few days. And that was a few days longer than a clean house, or clean kids, or clean dishes.

Frustration comes as we see others acquiring recognition, and we feel more and more insignificant. We're out of the spotlight. Life seems to be rushing by.

A lack of appreciation and affirmation in our lives will also produce frustration. The house may actually look worse at the end of the day than it did at the beginning, and our husbands may wonder what we've been doing with ourselves!

Our frustrations will differ depending upon how many children we have, whether we work outside the home, whether we get support or not from our husbands, and how our own personalities perceive the situation. I have noticed that we all loosely fit into two categories. Some of us are "do-ers" and some of us are "be-ers."

A do-er is apt to be a person who is an overachiever. Perhaps she is accustomed to a successful career with recognition, satisfaction, and approval, as well as salary. All of a sudden she is thrust into the home, coping with kids, when she is used to a more high-powered existence and used to running on all cylinders. In her situation as full-time mom, frustration comes because she sees little success or progress on a daily basis.

There's a sense of feeling overwhelmed with things that have no "lasting value"—like the twenty-two loads of wash I had in one week; like the one-hundred and forty-four diapers that I changed in one week; like the runny noses that are dirty five minutes later; the food that's cooked with only scattered dirty dishes to show for it.

The do-er's tendency is to equate progress with self-worth. In the home with young ones, there is often little progress to see. I've wondered about how much we talk about material progress and accomplishments in this century. In a sense, progress seems to have become an idol. Progress is considered to be inherently good.

A subtle erosion of self-esteem for the do-er occurs because it often takes everything she's got just to get through the day maintaining the status quo. According to the logic of the day then, what she's doing is not particularly worthwhile, and consequently she's not particularly worthwhile. The do-er's self-image plummets as she experiences this feeling of lack of accomplishment.

Even though she may be totally committed to the principles of full-time motherhood, it is still hard for her to bring her emotions in line with her convictions. Even for the do-er who also works part-time or full-time outside the home, frustrations loom over her. Perhaps she's a perfectionist, and here she is juggling two worlds—career and family—and not feeling particularly successful at either. Also, by trying to succeed in both worlds, she is frustrated because so little time is left over for herself.

Another problem for the do-er is the inclination to overcommit herself in community work. There is a continual demand for volunteer workers, and we're often flattered when the call comes from a friend who says, "There is a desperate need for someone to...and we know you would be perfect for the job." The tyranny of overcommitment can cause more frustrations as the do-er realizes she is not doing *anything* as well as she feels she can.

The be-er, on the other hand, may have an easier time being in the home full-time because of her personality. She is apt to be less driven than the do-er and is more easily. able to relax and enjoy the moment. The frustration for the be-er may come in just coping with the overwhelming demands of mothering. While she won't struggle as much with a lack of progress as the do-er does, she will struggle with the constant burdens of her never ending tasks.

The be-er may be just fine until a friend calls her and says, "What's on your schedule for today?" Panic may set in because she doesn't have a set of goals for her day. Her sense of frustration will come as she compares her lifestyle to that of her do-er friend, and she feels bad because she's not as organized and doesn't seem to accomplish as much as others do.

A be-er who works outside the home as well as mothering may actually be more relaxed than the do-er because of lower expectations on herself. However, there will still be the frustration of not being able to be the mother or the professional she desires because of the many conflicting commitments on her job and with her family. In addition, she may find that she has a difficult time focusing on any one project all the way through to completion.

It's interesting to see these personalities in our children. Often we will have one child who is very relaxed and plays happily by himself. This child is happy as a be-er. Another child may thrive on projects and plans and have a hard time playing alone. She is a do-er. Recently I awoke very early to find one of my seven-year-old twins propped up in bed, writing furiously on a legal pad.

"Susy, what are you doing up so early?" I asked.

"Why, Mommy, I'm making a list for you of all the things you need to get done today." That's my do-er daughter.

We see these differences in our marriages, too. Sometimes it works well if a be-er marries a do-er. That in itself can cause conflict, but if the differences are recognized and appreciated, and we learn how to mesh them together, a much greater balance in the marriage and the home can occur.

Although generally we will all fall into these two categories, some moms may be a blend of the two. At different times most of us will exhibit both traits. Neither of these personality types is better than the other; they are merely different. The benefit lies in recognizing who we are and understanding what might cause our frustrations. It's dangerous to compare ourselves with one another. As we attempt to cope with frustrations common to all mothers, we need to see ourselves as God sees us. He has made each of us uniquely different, and it is helpful to learn to appreciate these differences. We must realize afresh that our self-worth is not dependent upon seeing material progress, success, or accomplishment each day. God's love for us is not dependent on how much we seem to get done or how successful we seem to be. He loves us just because we are His, and nothing we do or don't do can change that.

So, in creatively dealing with frustration, it really does help to recognize whether we are be-ers or do-ers. This enables us to see why certain things frustrate us. Often just knowing why we respond the way we do comforts us.

"Imagined perspective" also aids in lowering the frustration level. Imagine yourself in five years looking back at this day, and you'll often find that what seems tremendously frustrating right now will in fact not be that important, given some time and some perspective.

It is also important to see these frustrations, though perhaps unpleasant for us right now, as a potential blessing from God. Often in these everyday situations, God teaches us more about Himself. In times of frustration, I have found it very comforting to curl up with one of the Psalms. They are full of frustrated pleas, and yet peace always is within reach as we focus on God's goodness and faithfulness. His joy is far greater than our frustration. He cares for us much the way any loving parent would care for his child. He's not frustrated with us. His love is characterized by perfect patience. So when those inevitable moments come we can be encouraged by meditating on His love for us.

> The Lord is gracious and merciful; slow to anger and great in loving-kindness. The Lord is good to all and His mercies are over all His works (Psalm 145:8-9).

Fatigue

A second cause of a plummeting self-image in young mothers is fatigue. Physical exhaustion, particularly for parents who are up a lot at night, takes a heavy toll. A friend with three small children recently said, "I can't wait until I have some free time and don't want to use it to take a nap!"

Not one of our five children was a sleeper. They were all colicky; and even though we tried every trick known to man, they didn't sleep through the night until they were nearly two. We counted once and realized we'd survived almost ten years without sleeping through the night. I remember thinking, *Lord, I have a glimpse of what it must be like to be in a concentration camp where they don't let you sleep. I can go without food, but I don't think I can go without sleep any longer.*

I recall getting up in the morning and praying, *Just please let me make it a couple of hours until somebody falls asleep.* There were times when I'd find myself nodding off in the middle of a story while trying to read to a two-and-a-half-year old. Several times I slept in the basement with my head under extra pillows so I would not hear children in the night. I knew they might fuss and be unhappy, but I also knew that if I didn't sleep I might not make it through the next day.

Fatigue caused by the routines of child care is quite different from fatigue caused by extra hours of work on an exciting project. The former fatigue is accompanied by depression; the latter by euphoria. One fatigue has resulted from maintaining, yet never completing, a final product. The other fatigue has resulted from tangible work on a tangible product—thus producing a sense of accomplishment making the fatigue seem "worth it."

Depressive fatigue occurs as we spend time each day and night in the routine of caring for our little ones. We are continually meeting their basic physical demands and these demands by definition are never satisfied once and for all. As children grow, they will be able to take care of their own physical needs, but much time in mothering small children is spent in dressing, feeding, changing, and potty training them. The same needs will begin all over again tomorrow. Our depression deepens because our tasks seem endless. We are bone tired. No end is in sight or will be for years.

When we are overcome by fatigue, two things are likely to happen. First, we tend to feel as if our brain is beginning to "atrophy." In our physical exhaustion, we turn our energies to the functional things we simply must do, and we just don't have the energy left over to stimulate our minds. My sister, who had three children in three-and-a-half years, once remarked, "I don't know how to carry on an adult conversation anymore!"

When we experience this, it helps to maintain a sense of humor, and realize that this state is only temporary. After all, our mental quickness *will* return once we get some sleep. I once paid a sitter to stay at my house so I could go to my neighbor's house and take a nap! Another time my husband Johnny and I went to a motel in town for a night so I could actually sleep one night through.

Humor helps. But so does seriousness. When you are able, why not read a little bit each day in something stimulating even if it's just this week's news magazine? It does wonders for one's self-image to focus mentally for a few minutes on something that has nothing to do with yourself or your family.

Secondly, fatigue often leads to emotional exhaustion. When we are very tired we need to be careful because we will often find ourselves saying things we will later regret or making decisions that are unwise. It's not a good time to get into a difficult discussion with your husband. It's too easy to respond out of fatigue rather than reason. I found that when I was extremely tired, it was best not to make any quick decisions or observations about important matters because my judgment was impaired.

As we experience fatigue, it's comforting to be reminded that God understands our exhaustion and that Jesus Himself has experienced everything that we will experience. He knew the depths of exhaustion (see Hebrews 4:15). He is the one who can give us grace and mercy to help in this time of need (see Hebrews 4:16).

In addition, exhaustion is a wonderful opportunity to catch a glimpse of what it means to be a servant. In serving small children, appreciation is not the norm nor is a sense of accomplishment. The motivation of our serving is simply the love we have for our children. Often the result of our serving is fatigue, yet we continue to serve because we love. We may not have warm *feelings* of love as we vacuum the dirty rug again, but we have the *conviction* of love. Love is, after all, a conviction and a commitment—which, when we put it into practice, will often but not always be accompanied by loving feelings. We serve out of our commitment, and in serving and in giving to our children we will receive joy. From our feeble attempts to serve, we will catch a glimpse of what it meant for God to give His Son to a life of service for us. During the exhausting period of motherhood, it's a good time to do a study in the Bible on being a servant. It will bring comfort and give us a vision for the tired days.

Thus, the first step to creatively coping with fatigue is simply to recognize fatigue. It's normal, and we all experience it. Be assured that God knows how we feel and that He has something special to teach us during this time.

The second step is also helpful, though: in the midst of a tiring day, attempt to complete one project. Clean out a closet, draw a garden plan, rearrange a bookcase, or study something interesting. As we do this, the depression that accompanies fatigue is lessened. Turning depressive fatigue into euphoric fatigue by seeing small accomplishments helps make the day go better.

During times of great fatigue, exercise takes on a new importance as well, because it brings the lift we so desperately need. With little children, the hours of five to seven in the afternoon and evening can be "arsenic hours." You either want to give it or take it! We are tired, the children are tired and hungry, the house is a mess, and we're trying to fix dinner. I used to try to go for a quick run just prior to "arsenic hour." I would grab a neighbor to watch the children, pull on my running shoes, and run for about fifteen minutes. I never felt like doing it, and often I went in tears of exhaustion, but it inevitably gave me the energy lift I needed to get through the next few hours. Regular exercise of some form is most crucial when we are physically exhausted. Getting out of the house one morning a week to play tennis really helped. Often I had to trade children with a friend, but knowing I had one morning to get away on my own helped me through the week.

Having one morning off each week is essential. It may take some creative child-care arrangements, but it is well worth the effort. The exercise and the break in routine are wonderful.

Eating properly is also important in the battle against fatigue. Sometimes moms are too exhausted to remember to eat anything other than those left-over peanut butter crusts. We can learn from the medical students who get very little sleep in those residency years. Good nutritional snacks help provide these students with energy and stamina. When we do have a spurt of energy, it's helpful to prepare some healthy snacks for those low times. Yogurt, fruit salads, hard-boiled eggs, cheeses, and granola bars kept in the refrigerator can provide a crucial lift during the day.

Sometimes we may fail to recognize that we are in a state of near collapse. A dull headache, dizziness, or near tears may indicate that it is time to call a halt to activity. Take the phone off the hook, put a note on the door, let babies play in their cribs, and crash for fifteen minutes. It is not a luxury; it is a necessity. When we experience fatigue, we also need to be reminded that this stage in our life is only temporary. The children will sleep eventually, and we will too. If we can recognize fatigue as normal and temporary, maintain a sense of humor, accomplish one small task, get regular exercise and good nutrition, we will go a long way toward preventing the depression that fatigue can so easily generate.

Guilt

A common problem for all mothers is the feeling of guilt. We feel guilty in parenting because we look at so many other mothers who *seem* to be doing everything right, and we know we aren't. We experience guilt because sometimes we actually find we don't even like our children! And, of course, we feel we should like our children all the time! Perhaps we have strong feelings of anger about our situation, and the anger brings on guilt, because we feel we shouldn't feel angry. Often our behavior is bad and we feel guilty. Guilt may be caused by any number of things but more often than not, it is the result of either unrealistic expectations or wrong attitudes and behavior.

Our expectations come from several different sources. They come from the role models that our parents provided. They are shaped by our husband's views, our in-laws, by our friends and by ourselves. For each person the sources will differ as will the degree to which these expectations shape our concept of how we are doing the job of mothering.

I have found that in my own life the greatest pressure I felt in terms of expectations came from myself. I was fortunate to be raised in a solid, loving Christian family and then to marry into one as well. I came into marriage and parenting expecting that because of my background I should certainly be able to do the job well. When all the kids arrived, I became tired, crabby, depressed, and I felt guilty because I was continually falling short of the expectations I had set for myself. *Susan, you don't have any excuses. You have been richly blessed.* I would often say to myself. The guilt that I felt from not living up to my own standards would grow. My husband and parents were supportive, but I was dissatisfied with myself. Slowly I began to realize that the expectations I was putting on myself were *not realistic!*

We should take a hard look at the expectations we have established for ourselves and determine if they are realistic ones. It may help to determine where those expectations have come from. Did they originate with our spouses, our friends, our family, or ourselves? It's helpful to sit down and have a talk with one's own husband and ask him what his expectation is of me and share my feelings with him. Together, as mates, we can discuss what is realistic and what isn't for our unique families.

It is important that we see what is right *for us*. There is a great temptation to look at *other people. She's got two children and she can really handle it. I'm about to die with one! What's wrong with me?* We are all made differently, and we have different levels of "cope-ability." We can learn from one another and be encouraged by each other. We can even share the discouragement we feel. However, we must be careful when we compare ourselves to others. We must remember that we are all made uniquely, and as we learn to appreciate these differences, we'll have a better outlook on ourselves.

Another common cause of guilt is our own wrong attitudes or wrong behavior. The Bible calls this *sin*. While that word may make us feel terribly uncomfortable, the best way to handle this problem is to boldly face up to the reality of our sin and seek forgiveness. Leave the arguing and the justifying aside for a moment. Sin is a universal problem. Often when we think of sin we think of the big obvious offenses like lying, stealing, or murder. Rarely do we think of envy, jealousy, or bitterness. However, on a daily basis it is more common for us to experience bad attitudes like these. Perhaps a negative attitude is expressed in envy toward a friend with small children who has household help when we don't, or bitterness because we had an unfortunate home life of our own, and therefore we don't have a good experience to emulate in parenting.

A common critical attitude experienced by mothers of small children is simply resentment—we resent being cooped up for another cold rainy day; we resent having to pay another pediatrician's bill rather than purchasing that new chair; we resent our frustrations, discouragement, and fatigue.

There have been many mornings when I awoke with a bad attitude about the day. I didn't want to get up, to speak to anyone, to take care of anyone. The prospect of a whole day ahead was actually depressing. I quickly learned that if I did not get that attitude straight right away, someone in my family was going to suffer! I would talk to God and tell Him exactly how I felt, ask His forgiveness for my bad attitude, and ask Him to give me a joy and a peace about the day ahead. Many times during the day I might have to go back to Him with the same requests. The amazing thing is that He never gets tired of hearing me, of forgiving me, and continuing to work His changing power within me. He doesn't say, "Oh, no, not Susan again!" He loves each of us so much, and He can use the children we have to mold us into the women He has created us to be. His understanding, His forgiveness, and His changing power have no limit.

When we experience these bad attitudes, we simply confess them as sin and ask God to forgive us and to change our attitudes. In God's Word He has promised us that as "we confess our sins, He is faithful and righteous to forgive us our sins and to cleanse us from all unrighteousness" (1 John 1:9). In addition, when God forgives, He forgets, and He casts our sins "as far as the east is from the west, so far He removed our transgressions from us" (Psalm 103:12). God does not just forgive us and leave us on our own to try to be better. He has given us the supernatural power of the Holy Spirit to change us (see John 14:26).

Sin is evident not only in our wrong attitudes but in our wrong behavior as well. There have been many times when I have wrongly lashed out in anger at one of my children when it was another child's fault or when I was in the wrong myself. I have found that I have to go to that child and say, "Honey,

Mommy was wrong. I should not have said what I did, and I need to ask you to forgive me. Will you forgive me?"

Then I ask the child to be with me as I pray and ask God to forgive me as well, and He does, and He restores the relationship. I feel it's not enough to say, "I'm sorry." I'm sorry does not elicit a response. "Will you forgive me?" does, and there's healing in forgiveness. The old classic *Love Story* had as its theme, "Love means never having to say I'm sorry." That may sound quite noble but actually nothing could be further from the truth.

In addition, it is absolutely necessary in marriage to be willing to swallow our pride from time-to-time and go to our mates and say, "Honey, I was wrong in what I said or did, and I need to ask you to forgive me." It is very tough to do this because we'd like to add our list of "buts": "But if you had…but if I hadn't…but if we didn't…." How easy it is to turn things around, blaming our partner. Even if our partner is partially at fault, the first step toward reconciliation may be when we ask forgiveness for what we did. A healthy marriage and a healthy family will be one where forgiveness—and asking for forgiveness—abounds.

Guilt produces many negative effects when we don't deal with it in a proper manner by confessing our sin and being forgiven. Sometimes when we do wrong, we may develop a tendency to blame others for what is our failing. "Well, if only my husband were more supportive, or if only my parents would help me, or if only we had more money…." We must be very careful that we don't attempt to throw off our own sense of inadequacy by blaming others. The "if-only" syndrome can lead to bitterness and self-pity.

It's easy to develop a really serious case of "poor me." When we feel the need for such a "pity party" approaching, we should tell God how we are feeling and ask Him to forgive us and to help us out of the mood. Take time to reach out and care for someone else. There are always people in worse situations than we are. Find someone who's lonely and invite her over. Take small children for a short visit to some elderly person. Give a friend in trouble a call. Have the children make cards for someone who is sick.

There are a large number of single parents in our communities trying to manage their children alone. Those of us who are blessed with two-parent families need to be sensitive to those around us to whom we can reach out. Single parents experience the same feelings in parenting that those with a spouse have. But they are often greatly magnified because the single parent faces them alone. It is nice to have the mother and her children to a family meal or on a family outing. Invite her to a party. Single parents need to be included in the lives of couples. As we reach out to them, we will receive encouragement in our own lives. Caring for others is the first step in the cure for self-pity.

When we find ourselves in the situation of blaming others or having a "pity party," we need to recognize these as common outgrowths of guilt and frustration. They are wrong, and the same principle applies in dealing with these sins as with any others: confess, receive forgiveness, and begin anew!

There is one other type of guilt that must be mentioned. This is "misplaced guilt" because it occurs when we feel guilty about something over which we have no control. Perhaps our child breaks a neighbor's window, and we blame ourselves for not having more control. Or a friend's marriage breaks up and we feel guilty because we were unable to help. This type of guilt is misplaced because it does not belong to us. In his book, *Parenting Isn't for Cowards*, James Dobson deals especially with guilty parents who should not feel guilty. We need to take care that we do not assume unnecesssary guilt. We already have enough that is valid.

As we experience God's forgiveness, and see Him wash away our guilt, we will also find that we will be able more readily to forgive others. We will experience the joy of seeing our guilt transformed into victory as God continues His process of molding us into the mothers He created us to be.

Failure

Closely related to the problem of guilt is the problem of failure. It is an all too common problem. We all experience failure.

Sunday morning arrives, and there are so many little people to feed, dress, and get to church on time, clean, and in good moods. By the time we catch everyone and get the car loaded, there are only three minutes left until church begins. Then on the half-mile ride to the church, the children fight over who gets to sit next to the window. As we arrive and race up the walk, one falls and skins a knee. Blood messes up the new pink Sunday dress. Another child won't go to his class. We now have grumpy, crying, and dirty children and are in a rotten mood ourselves, and in of all places—church! What failures we feel like.

While there are multitudinous reasons for a sense of failure in all of us, three are generally experienced by mothers of small children. Attempting the unrealistic will often result in failure. Perhaps you planned a day of volunteer work at the school, of cleaning house, and of shopping. Then you topped off your day with a dinner party in the evening. By the time the dinner was prepared, it was awful. You felt embarrassed and a failure as a hostess. Probably in retrospect you'll see that trying to pack so much into one day was unrealistic. When any of us plan our days, we often forget to allow time for unexpected emergencies. With small children dictating how we spend a good portion of our time, we do not have the control that we would have in a more predictable occupation. Children are unpredictable, and we need to allow time for flexibility.

Second, we experience failure because we make poor decisions. When my twins were turning three, I thought it would be great fun to dress up as a clown at their birthday party. I was so excited and so sure that this would be the best birthday party ever. As the other two- and three-year-olds arrived, I appeared in full costume complete with makeup to surprise my own twins and their little friends. The children took one look at me and burst into tears! They were scared to death, and the party was a disaster. I had made a poor decision. These children were too young for clowns. I was so embarrassed and felt like a real failure.

A third cause of failure often falls in the category of sin. When I looked back at my own role of parenting and I experienced frustration, fatigue, and guilt, I saw that I was failing in so many ways as a mother. I didn't like it. Yet as I saw failure and began to think about it over a period of time, I realized that one of my real problems lay in the area of pride. I found that I had a great deal of pride because generally I had been successful in most things in my life. And then I had kids!

I have seen many unpleasant things about myself as I have attempted to raise five little people. I have failed repeatedly, and yet it has been these failings that God has used in my life to teach me that my real problem has been the sin of pride. It became clear that my self-image had been largely determined by my pride in who I was. Thus, when I fell short of my prideful expectations, my self-image had plummeted, and I felt utterly defeated and insignificant. My attitude of pride did not allow a lot of room for failure or weakness. Thankfully, I have begun to realize that as I experience failure and my pride is chipped away, God has been teaching me a greater lesson about my self-worth and about His love for me. I needed to recognize my sin of pride (when that was the real problem) and ask God to forgive me. Doing this has enabled me to begin to understand that His love and His approval of me is not based on the job I do as a mother, but is based on the fact that I belong to Him.

The sin of pride creeps up in many ways in each of our lives and will continue to do so as long as we live. Growth comes in learning how to recognize wrongful pride and in asking God to forgive us and to teach us.

It's indeed a shame that failure itself has such a negative connotation. We are afraid of failure even though it can teach us so much. We are afraid for our children to fail. We often don't accept failure on the part of our mates. But it is clear that failure often provides us with our opportunities for growth. And the refusal to face failure often cripples us, denying us the chance to mature and succeed.

Sometimes our own fear of failure will prevent us from taking good risks, attempting something new. Perhaps you've been asked to teach a class, and you'd like to; but you've never done it. And because you are afraid to fail, you turn down the opportunity. What a tragedy! We should never allow fear to prevent us from attempting new challenges. There is always an element of fear in anything new, which is normal. This fear can point us to Christ. When we are afraid we are more likely to look to Him for help. When we are comfortable in everything, it is easy to do things in our own strength relying on our own confidence rather than on the power of Christ. We all need new challenges to grow, and we must not permit the fear of failure to hold us back.

Acknowledging failure will also enable us to turn an unpleasant situation into an opportunity for growth. What did I learn about my disastrous birthday party? I learned to be careful about frightening small children. I learned to study and think through what would appeal to children of a specific age rather than what I think would be fun. In acknowledging my sin of pride, I am beginning to understand better God's unconditional love for me.

When we ask ourselves and our children, "What can we learn from this failure that will help us in the future?" then we will inevitably benefit. As we begin to see failure as a positive step in growth, we will be able to take a bit of the sting of humiliation out of the failure and add a bit of hope for a long-term positive lesson.

I have a big Golden Retriever dog whose name is Duchess. She is my biggest fan. When I'm a bad mother she doesn't care. When I look terrible, it doesn't matter to her. When I fail at something important, it makes no difference to her. She keeps wagging her tail and loving me. She's never in a bad mood. She doesn't "talk at" me all day. She just loves to be in my presence. She keeps me company and she comforts me! Even as I write, she's curled up at my feet cheering me on!

Pets are a wonderful, practical way to provide companionship and to build up fragile egos. When I was a child, I also had a dog. I'd tell him all my problems, and I'd go to him when I felt no one loved me. He was a great comfort. Having a pet for a friend can be wonderful for children. I especially recommend them if you have an only child. For any child or adult, a pet can be a gift from God (who unconditionally approves of us; though He does not always approve of what we *do*) to help in soothing the pain of failure and in building up our self-image.

Finally, it is crucial to have a sense of perspective about our failures. Certainly, not all failures are caused by sin. Once some time passes, and we recover from the embarrassment or agony of failure, the incident will not appear to be nearly as shattering as it does in the midst of defeat. When we accept failure in ourselves and allow our children and our spouses to fail, we are acknowledging that we are all going to fail. Since it is in failure that we learn some of the greatest lessons in life, our failings need not overwhelm us. Instead we can realize anew that our self-worth is not determined by our success in living.

Being a good mother won't make God love me any more. Failing miserably will not take His love away. Running an organized home does not make me a more significant person. Juggling a career and a family with success will not impress God. God loves me just because I am His, and nothing can make Him love me any more. His love is already perfect.

Coping with my failures has made me aware of the danger of pride in my life. Facing your failures will perhaps show you something different. As we see failings in ourselves and others, we need to deal with them honestly, see them as potential blessings, and use them as great opportunities for growth.

Frustration, fatigue, guilt, and failure are all interrelated. Each of these agents work together to bring about a feeling of low self-esteem in mothers with small children. When we are able to see these feelings as normal—experienced to some degree by almost everyone in similar situations—we can take great comfort in knowing that we are not alone. When we want to be a "run-away mom" we will remember that others have felt this way, too.

Great joy and growth comes as we see these feelings not as enemies but as God's agents to lead us into a deeper relationship with Him. Our self-worth should be determined only by God's great love for us, which is constant and never changes. We can't take it away, improve upon it, or make it more. His love for each of us is already the most it can ever be!

Focus Questions

Meditate on Psalm 139.

1. Which cause of a low self-image is most true in my life right now?
2. What might God say to me if He were sitting here with me now?
3. What two specific, creative steps can I take this week to ease this problem and turn it into a positive growth experience?

Meditate on Ephesians 1:17-20, turning it into a personal prayer for yourself.

THREE

SEEING LIFE IN SEASONS

My teenage daughter came to me in tears one night because she felt lonely, left out at her high school, and with no friends she could really talk to who would understand her. It immediately brought to mind—with a flashback of pain—my own memory of going to my mother's side in tears because I wasn't a part of the "in crowd." I felt ugly, and I wasn't popular. Unlike my daughter who is beautiful, very bright, and a varsity cheerleader, I felt unattractive, with thick glasses and braces on my teeth, not terribly bright, and too uncoordinated to be a cheerleader.

No matter what assets they have or don't have, all teens go through a time of feeling lonely, left out, and not quite acceptable. There's also the tendency to think they are the only ones with these feelings. It's just that season of their lives. The difficult thing for the one experiencing it is that it seems these feelings will never go away. There's a sense of aloneness and hopelessness. They fear they'll always be this unhappy.

We all need to see our lives in terms of different seasons. We have friends who have a fourteen-year-old son. He's grown eight inches in the last year. He's bright, handsome, and has a great disposition. He doesn't know it yet. He went snow skiing recently, and no matter how much private instruction he had, he simply could not catch on. His body had grown so fast in such a short period that it had not had time to learn to be under control.

You can probably imagine how embarrassed he was before his friends. Fortunately, a wise adult took him aside and said, "Son, you will learn to snow ski one day, and you will be a good skier. What you are experiencing is normal. It's not your fault. You're not weird. The other kids will go through this rapid growth, too. It's an awkward time, but it will pass."

One month when the children were all small, we had three

cases of chicken pox, two ear infections, one case of bronchitis, and three cases of the flu. My eight-year-old son said to me, "Mommy, in your day people died of the flu!" At that point I thought I might die from nursing sick children! Young children get sick, and sometimes you wonder what it's like to have everyone in the family healthy at the same time.

Whether it's as a teenager, an adult, or a young child, what we all need to see is that many of our present difficulties in life are temporary. They are usually normal—experienced by the majority of people in similar situations—and they will soon change with the passage of the particular season that we are in.

Each season in our lives will be characterized by at least three frustrating traits. *First, a season will have, especially during its most difficult moments, a sense that "this will never end."* The young child is afraid he will *never* learn to read, the teenager fears she will *never* be popular, and the mother, overwhelmed by small children up at all hours, wonders if she will *ever* be energetic and rested.

A second trait common to each season is the tendency to feel that we are alone in our frustration. A new mother, feeling resentment at the demands on her time that this much-longed-for baby has brought into her life, experiences an additional burden of guilt for her surprised new feeling. She is sure no other mother has felt this way. A young child excluded from two neighborhood friends' clubhouse feels devastated and alone in her exclusion. It would never occur to her that her mom and dad once had a similar problem when they were kids. A teenager struggling to be accepted often thinks he's the only one who doesn't like the way he is. A sense of aloneness during the challenges of life is a common experience almost everyone faces at almost every stage.

Third, we tend to magnify small problems into major crises. That eighteen-month-old child who cannot have a cookie just prior to dinner, may throw a tantrum that you are sure the entire neighborhood hears. If a friend were to walk into this hysterical scene, the commotion might appear to be grounds for child abuse. This is not a major crisis to the parents, but it is to the child who wants his own way. Stand firm! It will pass, and he will learn he can't always have what he wants.

A teenager will be sure that she is "doomed for life" if she does not get invited to the homecoming dance. A conscientious young mother fails to recognize an emotional need in one of her children. When the child experiences some minor difficulties, the mother, in her despair, may fear she has damaged her child for life! It is very easy for us all to see a small problem as a tremendous crisis.

Each of these three traits is caused in part by a loss of perspective in our situations. As we grow and look back in our lives, many of the things that seemed so crucial do not seem as important given some time and some wisdom. What makes the difference is simply perspective. Young mothers especially need this, and that is why it is helpful to see our lives in terms of different seasons. As we look at our lives in seasons, we will acquire a sense of hope in the future and the ability to appreciate the unique joys inherent in the season at hand.

Before taking a look at the different seasons we experience as moms, it's helpful to get a sense of God's perspective. No matter where we are in life, God is in control. Psalm 31:3 says, "Thou art my rock and my fortress; / for Thy name's sake thou wilt lead me and guide me." When we are confronted with life's challenges in each season, it is easy to have all of our attention focused on the problems. We lose sight of the fact that God is in charge, that He loves us, and that He will see us through. In a sense, we must turn our eyes away from the challenge at hand and put them back on God—looking to Him for guidance, comfort, and peace.

God has a purpose and a plan for every phase in my life. He is the master of what goes on. He has called me to be exactly where I am, and He will teach me in every season. Psalm 32:8 says, "I will instruct you and teach you in the way which you should go; I will counsel you with My eye upon you." In each season there are many things to learn and to enjoy. God will use the difficulties and the successes to enable us to grow in our relationship with Him.

Expectancy plays a large role in enabling each of these periods to facilitate growth. As I expect to learn from God in each season in my life, I will be more open to His gently teaching me more about Himself. In the process I will learn more about myself. We can have confidence that each season indeed will be one of growth.

Finally, as we walk through these different times in our lives,

God will give us the resources to enjoy them. We are not meant only to endure toddlers but to enjoy them. Of course there will be periods in each season of sheer endurance, but overall one's attitude should be that of enjoyment.

As we look to God in each season, confident that He does have a special plan for our lives, and as we have expectant hearts eager to learn what He has to teach us, we will discover that each season will bring unique blessings to us and to our families.

Newlyweds to Newly Parents

Newlyweds have adjustments. Newly retired couples have adjustments. A new widow has adjustments. We all have adjustments as we experience change. Seasons by definition are begun by change. Getting married is a big change for two people used to living and functioning simply as individuals. Expectations represent one area in which changes will occur within a new marriage. We all come into marriage with differing expectations. Often these expectations are shaped by our own upbringing. We marry perhaps expecting our husbands to respond in the ways in which our own fathers did, and we may be in for a big surprise.

My cousin Caroline has been married for six months. She tells how when she was small, on special occasions, her dad would do the grocery shopping. When he did the shopping it meant special treats for the children and surprises for mom. It was a big event to meet dad when he returned from the grocery store with pockets of sweets. Not too long after they were married, Steve volunteered to grocery shop. Caroline waited expectantly for the goodies she was sure he would bring. When he returned and proudly displayed his "find" of collards and turnips with other healthy food, her face fell. She was disappointed. He was disappointed. He thought he had done such a good job, and still he had not pleased her. Their expectations were simply different, and it provoked one of their many newlywed adjustments.

Another adjustment that many newlywed wives experience is the shock of fleeting romance. Often used to being courted and romanced before the wedding, they expect it to continue after the marriage. Alas, husbands seem to lose all sense of romance and the wives wonder what happened to their "Prince Charming"!

The first few years of marriage are a season of learning how you fit together, of leaving your parents, or if you are older, of leaving your independence and establishing a oneness. It can feel awkward or it can be blissful. In this season it is important to have a sense of humor and to see this season as one of *realization*. It's a time of realizing how we are different, how we are alike, how our expectations must change, and how we can become one.

Pregnancy is another season. Pregnancy affects women in different ways. Some blossom and feel wonderful. Some are sick as dogs. I always felt terrible. I remember driving down the street in my car with two toddlers and stopping at a stop sign to open the door and throw up. Pregnancy, I'm sorry to say, is an unpredictable time. I found that it was a time when it was best for me not to make any important decisions or judgments. I was tired, and my emotions weren't trustworthy. Pregnancy often makes us act out of character, and it's a time when husbands need to be especially sensitive to us, extra loving, and not take us too seriously when we fly off the handle. The baby will come, and our sanity will return. Our uneven disposition is not intentional. Hormonal changes do crazy things, and often we can't help it. One husband shared that he found it difficult to always find his wife tired and that he tended to feel sorry for himself. It helped him to remember that she was carrying his baby and that his part was to be patient and considerate.

Once the first baby does arrive, we have entered a new season with a bang! We soon wonder in amazement how one person can cause so many changes in a family. A friend once told me that when her first child arrived it seemed as if someone had thrown a completed jigsaw puzzle into the air. All of the pieces of her life and marriage that had been so carefully put into place fell someplace else, and it was like starting over again. Contrary to the image portrayed by all of the greeting cards with photos of sweet, clean babies and adoring parents, having babies is not romantic! It's work.

In one of the child development classes in our local high school, the teacher has a unique way of communicating the realism and responsibility of parenting to her students. Each student is given a five-pound bag of flour to care for during one week. The "baby" can't be left alone. "Baby sitters" must be found. If the "baby" is neglected and the flour bag torn, the student gets a low grade! In this humorous exercise, the students get a glimpse into the reality of parenting.

The baby ushers in a period of new adjustments. If the wife has quit working, she has to adjust to "just" being at home. This is hard for some, thrilling for others. If she's still working, she now has to balance the needs of yet another person in the family. This takes more planning and more sacrifices on the part of both husband and wife. I thought that the first child was the hardest because I went from great freedom to being really tied down.

Of course, there are several aspects of this season that make all the adjustments, all the work, and all the sacrifices more than worth the effort. As parents we have a special privilege of knowing God from two perspectives. As we lovingly hold our babies in our arms we catch a glimpse of how God, our Father, loves us. Our feelings as earthly parents cannot compare to the love God has for us, and yet our parental emotions are a wonderful taste of what His love for us is like.

At the same time, we catch a picture of what it means to be the child our Heavenly Father loves. Seeing the parallels in my life as parent and child to my relationship with God as a child has given a deeper appreciation of the wonder of God's love. I reflected on this years ago in my journal:

> When I hold my seven-month-old baby in my arms, I learn so much about adoration. How she adores me. The smile she gives me as I nurse her says, "I can do no wrong." My presence brings her complete joy. Her little face breaks into a smile when I walk into her room. She has no fear. She is peaceful in my presence. She is not afraid that I will forsake her or treat her poorly. She just adores me. She would love for me to hold her twenty-four hours a day. She forgives me and seems to forget when I unintentionally bump her. She trusts me completely.
>
> Couldn't I but give to my Heavenly Father some of this pure adoration and trust that my child gives to me? How her love fills my heart with joy. Couldn't I praise my Heavenly Father in this way! From her I catch a glimpse of what it must mean to trust and adore my Heavenly Father.
>
> As I love her so much and yet so imperfectly I'm overwhelmed by how much my Heavenly Father must love me. Her bald fuzzy head is mine. Even her birthmark is precious. I love her because she's mine. God loves me because I'm His—not because I'm blonde or tall or nearsighted, but just because I'm His—just as she is mine.

Thank you, little one, for what you teach me about my Heavenly Father.

Becoming parents allows us to learn much about our relationship with God. Our children are babies for only a brief time and this is indeed a season of wonder. Babies wonder as they look around them. Their faces radiate a sense of awe as they take in their surroundings. The simplest things bring them joy. Sunlight on a crib sheet, shadows on a curtain, music from a toy, the coos of a mother trying to communicate—seem to be fully and wondrously noticed by an infant. But the season of new parents can be a season of *wonder* for us as well. It can be a season in which we are reminded to sit back and observe all that God has done for us. It is a season in which we relearn how to enjoy the simple beauties of life. As we see the world through our infant's eyes, it's a good opportunity to recapture the wonder and to appreciate the beauty around us that we have perhaps taken for granted.

Toddler Years

One day a good friend called and said, "Can I drop by for a visit?" "Sure," I replied, "but you'll have to sit on the floor in the bathroom with me because I'm trying to potty train the twins."

For several years I felt I was majoring in wiping bottoms or tying shoes. The girls would get so excited when they actually went in the potty that they brought it to me wherever I was to show me. They weren't the least bit bashful about greeting neighbors with their bare bottoms and latest achievements.

Toddler years are the most trying and the most precious. They have so much energy. When I get to heaven, I'm going to ask God why He gave small children so much energy and parents not enough. I'm also going to ask Him why boys love to wrestle all the time. My boys came into this world wrestling. As toddlers they turned our home into a training camp! Their energy knew no bounds. At ten and twelve, they still love to wrestle, and now they have a regular round robin with their seven-year-old sisters after dinner each night. It's a phenomenon I've noticed in most boys that I still fail to understand.

During the toddler years we experience three unique challenges: the challenge of teaching obedience, the challenge of harnessing energy, and the challenge of maintaining control.

The battle of the wills is in full force during the ages of two and three. It is the season of the child's attempt to determine who is in control. Training the toddler to obey is an exhausting, often unrewarding challenge.

My husband asked, "Honey, what did you do today?" I replied, "I disciplined toddlers all day." At times we feel we deserve the title "meanest mom in town"! While teaching obedience is not fun, it is necessary during this season. As the small children learn to obey their parents they are not only being prepared for living in the world, but they are also being taught the principles that will help them learn to obey their Heavenly Father.

Hand-in-hand with this challenge of obedience is the challenge of harnessing the incredible energy that these toddlers have. Children don't learn to walk, they learn to run. They are like bowling balls loose on paths of destruction. The season of toddlers is not a good time to decide to redecorate your house! Once when the twins were two-and-a-half, they went through the house and unscrewed and removed all the lamp switches. We never found them and had to take every lamp to the shop. During cold winter months it takes real creativity to know what to do with that energy. I often would pack the kids into the car and head to the closest mall to ride the "moving steps" (escalators) for half an hour. It was a small break in the long day and helped to unleash some of the energy.

Toddlers make mothers feel they have lost control of their families. They give orders like generals! They are unpredictable, and they constantly interrupt plans. The do-er mom who awakes in the morning with a mental list of what she hopes to accomplish during the day had better lower her expectations because she's in for disappointment otherwise. Toddlers demand a great deal of flexibility on the part of their mothers. One time, a do-er mother of three toddlers who had been totally frustrated suddenly appeared to exhibit more of a sense of peace in her life. When asked by her friends what "miracle" had taken place, she simply said, "I lowered my expectations for each day!"

Although we certainly struggle to maintain obedience, energy, and control, we also have the special opportunity to enjoy the uniqueness of this season. Whereas small infants represent a season of wonder, toddlers represent a season of *discovery*. A toddler's curiosity is never satisfied, and it can get her into all sorts of trouble. Once I found Libby on top of the kitchen table eating sugar from the sugar dish. When that ran out she simply continued with the salt thinking it was the same. Her gagging, spitting, and screaming brought the rest of the family hurrying to the scene of the crime where we had a hard time trying to comfort her instead of laughing at her!

It is during this season of discovery that we moms are reminded to be observers ourselves. We will enjoy this season much more as we observe what our children do and what they say. They will say and do the funniest things; and once they've left this season, these humorous things will never be repeated. As we observe, it's fun to write down some of the cute things children say.

At her first view of the ocean, Libby said, "It's too full, Mommy. I think we ought to let some of it out." When asked what Superman does, Chris responded, "He flies in the sky talking to Jesus and God."

I would not have remembered these moments if I had not quickly written them down. These quotes will become special to us as our children grow up. Also, as the children grow they love to hear us tell them the things they used to say or do when they were younger. It's a treat to record these "sayings and doings" in a child's book or mother's journal and pull it out to share on each child's birthday. Taking pictures of ridiculous happenings also helps us to be observers and therefore enjoy this season. Photograph the crazy things, the dress-up parties, the meal fights, not just the Sunday specials. These pictures will become treasures and bring to mind forgotten incidents.

Hank Ketcham, who is the cartoonist for "Dennis the Menace," is a great observer of children. His cartoons are so funny because they are derived from ordinary humorous things that children say and do. One of my favorites is a picture of Dennis angrily going upstairs to his room, turning to his amazed mother and saying, "How come I have to take a nap when YOU'RE the one who's tired?"

We may not be cartoonists, but we could do research for Ketcham as we learn to observe. Taking time to observe will be easier for be-ers than do-ers. The do-ers must remind themselves to take time to enjoy the moment and not always be thinking ahead to something that needs to be done. The season goes by too fast, and it's too easy to look back and wish we'd taken more time to enjoy it. When you're in the midst of diapers and crying babies, you think it'll never end; but when they go to school, you wonder in amazement at how fast the time went.

The Kids Grow Up

Allison has a dental appointment this afternoon, John has basketball practice, Christopher must be picked up from a friend's house, and Susy and Libby have a birthday party—all in a two-hour span. My place of residence has become an old 1978 station wagon!

As the school-age season begins, new and different challenges present themselves. Whereas mothers of toddlers and babies suffer from physical exhaustion, mothers of teens and preteens are most likely to become emotionally exhausted. With small children it is the physical demands that are overwhelming. When children begin to grow up and are able to take care of many of those physical needs, the emotional needs become more obvious. One child doesn't have a special friend, another has too many. One child wants to do every activity available, another has to be pushed to participate in even one social activity. Because our children are different, they will have different needs; and it's easy for the mother to become overwhelmed as she attempts to meet all the needs.

There are three challenges in particular for the mother during this season of maturation. First, the children are becoming increasingly independent. As we train our children, it is important that we slowly encourage them step by step to become independent. This is a gradual process. It involves learning personal responsibility, making wise decisions, and carrying through on commitments. Often our children believe they are ready for certain things before we feel they are. Growing together in independence is a challenge for parents and for teens.

Making choices is another challenge that parents and growing children face. When we are at home with toddlers, our choices center around which activities within the home to do next. Shall we color or make play-dough? Although we don't appreciate it at that time, we do have some control over our lives and the lives of our children. With active older children, the choices become more numerous. One wants to play basketball, another soccer, another wants ballet lessons. It is so easy to become overwhelmed with opportunities, and it takes careful evaluation of family needs to determine which choices to make.

In addition to the challenges of growing independence and of making choices is the difficulty of helping our preteens and teens maintain a positive self-image during the trying adolescent years. Self-identity is very fragile, and peer pressure is enormous. I've often wished we could bottle some of the self-assurance of the two-year-old and save it for an injection when she reaches thirteen! During this unique season of watching the children grow, it is important that we remember that they are God's children. He loves them even more than we do. We cannot possibly meet all of their needs. I once prayed, *Lord, there are so many needs among my little people. I cannot meet them all. I ask you, Father, who knows their needs far better than I, to meet their needs today through others—perhaps a neighbor, a friend, a teacher, an achievement, a sibling. Thank you, Lord, that you aren't limited to using me to shape them and encourage them.*

During this period, we have the unique opportunity to gently point them to God to meet their needs. My teenage daughter recently had to decide between two conflicting activities at school. I honestly did not know which she should choose. We talked, then prayed together about her options asking God to show her which was the better decision. He did show her, and my faith was encouraged as I saw Him at work in her life. Her faith is growing as she looks to Him more and to her parents less for guidance. He is faithful, and He knows what is best for each of our children.

Thus, in order to genuinely appreciate the uniqueness of this season, we must first remember that these are God's children. Second, we must help them turn to Him for guidance. Third, we must simply enjoy the companionship of our children as we spend time with them. As our children leave toddlerhood, we can find tremendous satisfaction in getting to know them as they grow into adulthood. There is a tremendous amount of pressure for us to fill our calendars with our own activities, for example, volunteer work, benefits, causes, parties, and the like, so that there is little or no time left to build friendships with our growing children.

Over and over again, we are forced into making choices about how we will spend our time and money.

We need to see these years as a great time to do things with our family. Naturally, the children will have a growing interest in their peers, and this is healthy; but there's also time—especially in the preadolescent years—for us to "hang out" with our kids. If we spend time talking and walking and playing with them in those years prior to the tumultuous adolescent years, it will make the adolescent years much easier to go through together.

Good friends of ours, Nancy and Jerry, moved to another town when their children were in junior high and high school. They are a couple who loved to entertain and were always the social leaders of the city. When they moved, they made a conscious decision not to run out and get involved in the social goings-on of their peers. They decided that since their kids would be at home only a few more years, they would spend their weekends focused on them. They realized they would have years ahead when the kids were away to get involved in the social circuit of their friends. They are now closer than ever before to their children, and their investment of time with them has paid tremendous dividends.

This year both of our boys played basketball. I think I've seen thirty losing games this season. Frankly, it gets awfully boring watching so many losses. But winning or losing, the boys still love it when I come. It is important to them. I have learned that from time to time I may need to make the choice to postpone some things I'd like to do in order to spend time with the children going to their sports events and their concerts during these post-toddler, preadolescent years.

I've also found those events to be a good time to be a "parent" to kids whose parents don't come. I never did meet either parent of one boy on my sons' team. His mother didn't live with the family, and his dad was too busy in his business to come to any games. The child really responded to hugs after each game and compliments of "you did a great job stealing that ball." With so many hurting families today, we need to make a special effort to reach out to the children of single parents or the children of parents who are "too busy."

The car has become a new educational institution. In a carpool, for instance, you can get a wealth of information. Young kids talk as if the driver weren't even there. You learn who likes whom, the latest bad words, and who did what naughty thing. The older kids are a bit more self-conscious; but sometimes when there's a crowd and they really get to talking, they momentarily forget you can hear. You learn things you'd never get your own child to tell you. Shuttling kids between their many activities can be a wonderful time of conversation and closeness. My friend Priscilla said that the one regret she had in her daughter's getting her driver's license was that she missed the talks they had when driving places. Cars can be a great time to talk and to listen. The audience is captive!

In this season of watching our children grow up, we begin to become aware that we do not have that many years left with them. As we look back over the past, we begin to realize just how fast time does go by. It drives a mother surrounded by toddlers crazy to hear a mom with older kids say, "Enjoy it, it goes by so fast." She's just trying to live through it! And yet as we come to the teen years we are amazed at how short the time is. Postponing some of our own interests and being with our kids as they experience the pain and the victory of growing up will enable us to build firm friendships with our children that will continue to grow in the seasons to come.

Alone Again

As the children begin to leave the nest, we enter another season. It's a time of letting go, and it can be harder on the mother than the dad, especially if she has poured her whole life into her children. As women, we need to be preparing ourselves for the children's departure from the time they are small. We should be developing interests of our own whenever time allows. We need to be praying and planning for new directions and perhaps new careers. When we are surrounded by babies, it is a time to put our interests and careers on the back burner. But as they reach school age, it's helpful, if we aren't already working outside the home, to begin to think about our next career—the one after child-raising. We need to take some classes, or explore the possibilities, so that when the children leave, we'll already have a plan. Even if we've worked all along, we need to make certain we don't underestimate this crucial adjustment.

I personally feel that if we can be at home when we are raising the children, it is best. If economic necessities dictate that we must work, perhaps we can work part-time or only when the kids are at school. When those kids hit the door after a long day at school, it makes a big difference to have mom there available to comfort any wounds, to hear about the day, and to carpool to all those extra-curricular activities. It may not always be possible, but the more it can be done, the better. Those days are numbered though. And as they come to an end, we need to have purpose and direction for our lives.

As we reach the season of being alone, we will discover a number of challenges unique to this period in our lives. One is that of emotionally "letting go" of our grown children. This can be particularly difficult if we live in the same town with our married children. It is hard but necessary to realize that we can no longer solve our children's problems. We must allow them to struggle and grow alone in their own family unit.

This season in life may bring a number of other challenges as well. There may be the challenge of having grown kids return home when we thought the nest was empty. There may be a challenge in adjusting to retirement or to poor health or to losing one's mate.

But not only are there challenges, there are tremendous blessings as well. The variety of life increases. When we have small children we spend most of our time with other parents in our own age group. When our children are gone we will have the time to be enriched by being with both younger and older people as well as by doing things with people our own age.

When we are alone again we also have the freedom to make choices we've not had. There is now time to pursue as individuals and as couples those interests that we postponed.

Finally, there is at last the freedom to have some solitude. In our solitude, as we look over our lives, we should be overcome with a sense of God's faithfulness. No matter what difficulties we have faced or what blessings we have received, the greatest joy comes as we see that God has indeed been there all along.

Overlapping Seasons

Most of us will never be in one season exclusively. We may find ourselves coping with teenagers and with toddlers at the same time. My friend Barbara has four children, ages seventeen, twelve, five, and three. She says that one of the biggest challenges has been continually having to shift gears mentally. It's quite a jump from struggling with college applications to riding tricycles. It is especially interesting when the big children and the small ones have immediate needs! A related challenge is finding fun things that the entire family can do together. The big kids would like to go out to an adult dinner, yet the little ones would ruin it!

On the blessing side, Barbara says that her older children are receiving great training for being parents themselves. It has been such fun for her to have older children to share in the joys of watching all the funny things the small ones do. In addition, the small children have built-in examples to follow. In a sense, they have their own ready-made youth ministry!

We may find ourselves dealing with a very ill parent and raising small children at the same time. In a situation like this, one of the greatest pressures is that of time. The emotional and physical needs of an ill parent demand much time. There is the tension of whose needs to meet first, your children's or your parent's. On the other hand, children living with an elderly or ill grandparent will learn much about the reality of aging and death in a loving context. They will learn compassion and caring. One young boy, after caring for his ill grandmother for several hours, remarked to his mother, "Mom, I did not realize what you had been going through." This whole family learned to appreciate one another in a deeper way.

When the seasons seem to overlap and we are confronted with a wide range of demands, we need to be reminded that God is still in charge, and that He will bring us through this time. Nothing during this "mixed-up season" will go to waste. We do not know what God has planned for our children or indeed for ourselves. Perhaps we have a child who will eventually work with the elderly as a result of growing up in a family with one. Perhaps we have a teenager who has needed to learn responsibility, and helping to care for a surprise new sibling has provided that opportunity.

God will use for the good everything that comes into our lives. He has promised us in Romans 8:28. "God causes all things to work together for good for those who love God, to those who are called according to His purpose."

Whatever "mixed-up season" we may find ourselves in, we can rejoice knowing that God is there too. He knows our needs, and He will meet them. Seeing life in seasons enables us to get some perspective on our lives. In every season there will be trials and joys. Hardly anything lasts forever. We need to see our life in seasons and rejoice in the season at hand. As we relax and begin to soak up the unique blessings of this particular season, we will begin to experience and to enjoy the richness of life.

Focus Questions

Meditate on Psalm 46.

1. What promises do I see in this psalm that encourage me in this season?
2. What special thing has God been teaching me during this season about Himself? About myself?
3. What practical steps can I take this week to enjoy the season I am in?

Meditate on Psalm 33 as a prayer of thanksgiving.

ESTABLISHING PRIORITIES THAT WORK

I curled up on the couch and pulled the coverlet around my shoulders in an attempt to ward off the damp chill seeping in through the windows. The rain lashed against the house in great fury. It was as if the harsh pellets of rain were intentionally trying to break through the walls of the house into the security of my home. The storm outside was but a reflection of the storm going on inside of me.

Another phone call had come in the middle of breakfast asking if I would do volunteer work at the school one day each week. I had already received requests to cook for a bake sale, be on a phone committee, serve as a room mother, teach Sunday School, and watch a neighbor's child. In addition, yesterday a friend had invited me to go with her to visit a museum. There were too many needs to be met and too many opportunities to take advantage of.

Confusion and frustration became my unwanted companions as I pulled the coverlet tighter around myself to lessen the impact of the storm outside. Gazing out the window at the tree branches blowing out of control, I realized that I, too, felt a loss of control and a lack of direction in my life. I had become merely a responder to the many demands and opportunities facing my young family. I no longer had a sense of being "in charge," of knowing what we should and should not do. There were too many options, too many needs, and too many voices telling me how we should live.

In our world of seemingly unlimited opportunity, it is difficult to determine how we should spend our time. Throughout history, everyone has had exactly twenty-four hours in each day—no more, no less. Yet the different possibilities on how to spend these hours has increased to the point of being contradictory. How do we determine what is right for us in the midst of overwhelming advice? Who is right? To whom do we listen?

Our lives can resemble a ship without a rudder on a turbulent sea. Without the rudder to respond to the changing weather patterns, the ship's action is controlled by the strongest current. When the rudder is in place and operating correctly, the ship will respond to the currents in a manner pleasing the sailor. We need a "rudder" in our lives to give us a sense of direction and control in responding to the opportunities around us.

We want guidelines that will work in all seasons and that are relevant no matter what we are going through or what ages our children are. We need some basic principles that will not overwhelm us or be just something else we have to live up to, but rather principles that will give us a foundation upon which we can stand and operate freely.

God's Principles

Because God made us, loves us, and knows us completely, we should look to His Word to find the principles that will give us a framework upon which to base our lives and those of our families. From those principles set forth in God's Word we will be able to adopt priorities that equip us to respond to all the demands around us. God's priorities will, in a very real sense, act as a rudder in defining who we are and thus give us the confidence we need to live in this complex world.

When we look to Scripture for guidance, it is helpful to study it from two different perspectives: direct teaching and personal examples. For instance, when we ask the question, "What should my first priority in living be?" the Ten Commandments may come to mind since they were the first laws given by God to His people through Moses. In them God's emphasis to His people was first and foremost that He was to be their only God (see Exodus 20:3). When Jesus Himself was asked what was the greatest commandment, He replied, "You shall love the Lord your God with all your heart and with all your soul and with all your mind"

(Matthew 22:37). This then has always been the most central Biblical teaching. From Moses to Christ over a period of approximately thirteen hundred years and now nearly two thousand years later: our first priority in life should be to love God.

Jesus loved His Father with all His heart and mind and soul. Thus He sought to do His will continually. In John 4:34, He says, "I have come to do God's will." Not only did Jesus do the will of His Father, He also spent time alone communicating with His Father. We have examples of His leaving the multitudes to be alone with God (see Mark 1:35, Luke 5:16). He also left His disciples by themselves so that He might slip away in worship with His Father. In the final hours of His life, we find Him again alone in the Garden of Gethsemane praying to His Father. His love for the Father knew no bounds.

So both in direct teachings and through personal examples, the Bible makes it clear that our first priority should be to love God. But Biblical instruction on priorities doesn't end there. As we look at the many different teachings and examples in both the Old and New Testaments, we will find that as believers our second priority should be to those around us, particularly our families. Jesus said that the second commandment was to "love your neighbors as yourself" (Matthew 22:39). Our families— husbands and children—are our most immediate neighbors. The lovely Old Testament story of Ruth's faithfulness to her mother-in-law, Naomi, is an example of the priority of a commitment to family.

Paul teaches clearly in his letters about the importance of caring for one's family (see 1 Timothy 3:12, 1 Timothy 5:8). One of Jesus' last acts before His death was an expression of provision, concern, and love for His mother. While on the cross He gave her into the care of His disciple John (see John 19:26). There are many other places in God's Word where we can see the principle of caring for our own immediate families presented as a priority for believers.

Third, there are many examples in Scripture that teach the importance of fellowship of a few close-knit friends. In the Old Testament, Moses had Aaron, Jonathan had David; and in the New Testament, Paul had Barnabas, Silas, and others. Jesus chose twelve men to be His closest friends. Out of those twelve He chose three, Peter, James, and John, with whom He spent much of His time. Proverbs teaches that "Iron sharpens iron. So one man sharpens another" (Proverbs 27:17). According to Paul, we are to "bear one another's burdens, and thus fulfill the law of Christ" (Galatians 6:2). Over and over again through examples and teaching, we find the importance of having a few close friends to whom we can be committed—friends who have a common faith in Christ and with whom we can share our hearts.

Finally, our fourth Scriptural priority should be to act as Christ's representatives in the work He has called us to. Colossians 3:17 says, "Whatever you do in word and deed, do all in the name of the Lord Jesus." In the book of Nehemiah, we see a lovely picture of many different Jews at work rebuilding the wall of the Temple. Some were repairmen while others built the new gates. Some kept guard while others worked. Whatever they did, they knew that their gifts, assets, talents, and contributions were being used to enable the whole body of Jews to live and worship without fear. As each person did his work properly, everyone benefited.

In Acts 1:8 we are challenged by Christ to be witnesses unto the remotest part of the earth. Clearly we are to be God's instrument in whatever profession He has placed us. We are to love and to serve those with whom we are involved, and in so doing to share the good news of Christ with them.

By the direct teaching of Scripture and by its many personal examples we should be able to highlight these four priorities in determining how we live our lives. But how do these priorities translate into practical guidelines for enabling busy mothers to be able to cope with the many demands upon their time? How do these priorities work out in the households of young children? Let's look briefly at each of the four priorities in light of their practical implementation in our homes.

Our Commitment to Christ

Christmas is two weeks from today. The workmen are hammering away, tearing my kitchen apart. The babies are screaming. Mom and Dad and Granny (age 89) are coming for the holidays. There's sawdust and dirt everywhere from construction. Christopher can't get Sesame Street clearly on TV. John can't find his other shoe. Allison wants to know why we don't have anything good to eat in the house. There are seven loads of wash to be done, and I'm hiding under the hairdryer—my noise suppressor—to talk to you, Lord. Lord, please help me not to let my desire for a neat house, organization, and calm determine my disposition. You know I like those things, but Lord, it's impossible. Please, Lord, help me walk with you above all those things today. Lord, help me keep my eyes on you.

This was a prayer of mine a few years ago. In the midst of diapers, schedules, and demands, it's easy to feel like that ship without a rudder, tossed freely by the greatest of winds. We need a rudder in our lives, someone more powerful than ourselves or our mates, someone with perfect love and forgiveness, someone who knows us and our children better than we ourselves do, and someone who has our best interests at heart. That someone is our Creator made known through His Son Jesus Christ.

Our first priority as moms must be to love God with all our heart, soul, and mind. We do this by growing in our relationship with Jesus Christ. Loving someone involves spending time with them. Because frustration, guilt, failure, and fatigue are prevalent in the season of young children, it is especially crucial that we set aside time each day to be alone with the Lord. It is in this "quiet" time that we experience a growing awareness of God's love for us, and we begin to love Him as well.

As we have seen, moms are continually required to give. We are continually meeting others' needs, and in the process we often find ourselves depleted. It is in a devotional time with the Lord that we can get our batteries recharged to be the mothers we want to be. My friend Shannon, who has two very active toddlers, says that the most important lesson in motherhood that she has learned is the necessity of setting aside time to be alone with God. She hates a messy house but once the boys are napping she has made the decision to ignore the mess, take the phone off the hook, and spend some time with God. She finds that as she meets with God, her perspective returns and she receives the power to carry on.

During our quiet time it is important to study a portion of Scripture and to pray. I discovered that looking at a portion of Scripture was like having a refreshing meal. The Psalms are an especially wonderful source of study. There are also numerous Bible study guides available from various publishers. The important thing is to have a plan of study for a quiet time. Taking notes will also cause the time to be more meaningful.

Prayer is the other aspect of our devotional time that is important. Prayer involves meditating or just listening to God. It also involves making requests. I've found the old "ACTS" formula helpful in my prayer life. "A" is for adoration, or a time of praising God for who He is. "C" is for confessing my sins. "T" is thanksgiving to God for specific things He has done. And "S" is for supplication, when we make our requests known unto God.

Susanna Wesley, mother of Charles and John Wesley, early pioneers in the Methodist movement, had seventeen children. You can imagine how difficult it must have been for her to find time or the place to be alone with God. It was said of her that when the children noticed their mom in the parlor with her large hoop skirt petticoats pulled over her head that they must not disturb her. This meant that she was praying!

In our "quiet times" as we study God's Word and as we pray, we will find ourselves encouraged as we learn to call on some of the promises in God's Word for us. Corrie Ten Boom once said that in the Bible there are seventeen thousand promises for us.[1] Mixing promises and prayer enables us to act on God's Word. For example, Philippians 4:6-7 has become a favorite of mine: "Be anxious for nothing, but in everything by prayer and supplication with thanksgiving let your requests be made known to God. And the peace of God, which surpasses all comprehension, shall guard your hearts and your minds in Christ Jesus."

As young mothers we are anxious about many things. But we can claim this promise in prayer:

> Lord, I'm worried about this sick child. I'm concerned about my good friend. I don't know how to handle this discipline problem with my two-year-old. I give you my anxious thoughts, and I ask for your peace to control my moods today. Help me to see your solutions to these problems!

In attempting to have a quiet time, we cannot wait until our homes are clean and we're caught up on things, because that time will never arrive. We need to simply set aside a time each day to be alone with God and consider these few minutes as the first priority in our day. As we spend time in prayer for our mates, ourselves, and our children, we can know that it's not futile wishing, but a turning over of our needs and desires to the God for whom nothing is impossible.

Our Heavenly Father loves us so much, and no matter who we are or where we've been or what we've done, He desires to have time with us. Our faith might be tiny. That doesn't matter. It's not the amount of our faith that's important; it's the object of our faith—the Almighty God. This Almighty God cares about our every need. He cares about the dirty house, the lonely child, the continually sick baby, our husbands' jobs, our neighbors' indifference. Nothing is too great or too small for His concern. As we take time to put Him first in our lives by taking all our cares to Him and by seeking to please Him, we will experience a peace that is deeper than any peace the world gives. When we pray, we'll see His power become great in changing us and our families.

One of the blessings of faith in Christ is that we recognize that raising kids isn't all up to us. We need the security of knowing Christ and of being able to spend time with Him on a regular basis, praying and reading His Word. His principles are timeless. They alone last through all social changes. They are applicable in every situation. And they provide us with a foundation upon which to raise our families. A vital relationship with Christ is like the rudder of the ship that keeps individuals and families on course no matter what the weather.

Our Commitment to Our Families

Several years ago, Sandy and Harry Chapin wrote a popular song titled "Cat's in the Cradle." The song describes a relationship between a son and a father. When the boy was small the father missed his son's first attempts to walk because he was away on business or busy paying bills. When the boy turned ten, the father had no time to play ball with him. He was too busy. The song ends with the father now retired, asking his son if he can see him. Alas, the son says he is too busy—he doesn't have time.

The Chapin's song describes a common problem of our day—lack of time to spend with our families. With all the opportunities available to us it's so easy to become a fragmented family with everyone going in a hundred different directions. Too often, meaningful conversation between family members gets lost; conversation is reduced to a totally superficial level. Who put the toys away? Did you make your bed? Did you brush your teeth? Who picked up the laundry? Who is paying the department store bill? Usually we slip into these superficial relationships within the family without even realizing that it is happening. We are all so busy and controlled by urgent needs that we neglect to listen and to share with one another on a deeper level.

It is vital to our families that we make our relationships with our mates our priority after our relationships with God. We have our mates living with us for a lifetime, whereas we have our children living with us for approximately eighteen years. Child psychologists have stressed that a child's security rests not as much in the fact that his parents love him as it rests in the fact that they love each other. The best gift we can give our child is the security of a loving relationship between his parents.

A good relationship between parents doesn't just happen. It takes work. More marriages die slowly from neglect than from great crises. We have a raspberry patch at our farm that produces the best red raspberries I've ever tasted. I've not spent much time weeding and fertilizing it over the past five years. At first the neglect wasn't noticeable. Each year, however, the berries have been fewer and more choked by honeysuckle. One year I made great strides in caring for the berries as I spent a week pulling honeysuckle. (My reward was a severe case of poison ivy.) The berries took on a new health temporarily, but alas, my attention wasn't constant. Now they look more faded than ever. My neglect over the years has been unintentional. There have just been too many other things to do. Neglect in a marriage works the same way. It allows the weeds of discontent to grow. It is essential that we work continually on our marriages and our families. It's too easy to neglect them. If they are not growing, they are dying even though the "disease" may not be evident yet. Husbands and wives must make a priority of spending time alone together. It is difficult for a relationship to continue to deepen unless we are willing to invest time in it. In this busy season we have a tremendous challenge to keep our marriages growing. But our family priority doesn't end with our spouse.

It is also essential to set aside time to be alone as a family, the whole family. Our children grow up very quickly. In the season of diapers, magic markers, and peanut butter crusts, we think there will be no end to the mayhem. Yet before we realize it, that two-year-old is sixteen.

Sometimes in our complex lifestyles we can arrive at the end of a week and realize upon reflection that the family has not all been at home together one night the entire week. This is especially true when the children get older and are involved in different extra-curricular activities. To prepare for those even busier years to come and to encourage family identity, it's helpful to plan one special family night each week. This is an evening to be alone together as a family to enjoy one another's company. Those nights need to be decided on in advance and put on the calendar.

When the children are small, it's fun to act out Bible stories, go on scavenger hunts, or watch old family movies. We've enjoyed cooking special dinners, bowling with tennis balls and empty plastic containers, and reading stories aloud. If the precedent of a family night is established when the children are young, it makes family nights with lively discussions more natural when the teenage years arrive.

Not only do we need time alone as families, but we also should attempt to have time alone with each of our children. The larger the family, the more complicated this will be. But the joy experienced as we continue to get to know each other is far greater than any sacrifice. It is important to plan some time alone with our children. It will not just happen. We have to help it happen. Every now and then it's helpful to "take stock" of my time with my children and ask the question, "Is there a child that I have not had some special time alone with recently?" How can I help this happen in the near future? The time does not need to be long, especially with small children. Sometimes a quiet ten minutes of coloring with a three-year-old will provide some much-needed attention. Perhaps reading a book together with another child can become your special time.

Once Christopher and I colored a T-shirt for him that said, "I'm special." He is my middle child and at the time was feeling more squashed than special by his brothers and sisters. That T-shirt became a treasure. Taking children out to lunch from school can provide a special date time with a parent. An early breakfast out with dad before work might be a rare treat.

We do not need to have extravagant outings or overdo home projects in an effort to have a meaningful time with our children. Turning away from the clutter of things and opportunities to the simple joys of life will be refreshing for all. A nature walk looking at what God has made, a time of singing together, or playing in a sandbox are examples of special times that will enable us to focus on the simple joy of being together.

As the children get older, longer stretches of time together with a parent can deepen relationships. When our children turned eight, I took them each away in turn for an overnight alone to some place special. There is nothing magical about that age. It just happened that Allison and I went away when she was eight, and it was so much fun that I decided to do it with each of the other children as well. Johnny does it when they are thirteen. These times of having one of my children to myself have been so precious and meant so much to me! Kids are such fun (at times!).

When they are approaching adolescence we also take them away for an adolescent weekend and listen to James Dobson's tapes together on preparing for adolescence.[2] Johnny takes the boys and I take the girls. It's great to have a third party, such as Dr. Dobson on tape, to respond to together in discussing the challenges of being a teen. Spending time playing with our children when they are small will open the door for them to talk to us when they hit the teen years. Birthdays, holidays, and vacations are excellent opportunities to plan some special events that will build family memories for your own families. *Family Celebrations* by Ann Hibbard is an excellent source of ideas.

It is interesting to note that a number of recent academic studies have confirmed these Scriptural truths. Columbia University spent a quarter of a million dollars to conclude that there is no second force in the eye of a child compared with the impact of his home.[3] In another study sociologists Nick Stinnett and John De-Frain surveyed one hundred and thirty strong families in Oklahoma. Their findings identify six qualities which strong families had in common:

1. Expressed appreciation

2. A lot of time spent together/things done together
3. Good communication patterns
4. A high degree of religious orientation
5. A high degree of commitment
6. The ability to deal with crisis and stress in a positive manner.[4]

Most of us will never spend as much time as we would like with our husbands or our children. We'll make great plans, have good intentions, then a crisis will arise and plans will fall apart. On the other hand, if we fail to plan time together, thinking that we'll have time when "things aren't so busy," we'll soon realize that life will always be busy. Just as we have goals in our professional lives to enable us to carry out professional priorities, we need family goals to help us keep our families in the place of high priority that God has called them to be.

Our Commitment to a Group of Close Friends

Recently a friend lost his job as a result of some personal problems. Sadly, none of his close friends even knew about the problems until it was too late. He had not been in regular contact with his friends. Had his friends been aware of the problems in his job earlier, perhaps their counsel, advice, and care could have aided in making some necessary crucial adjustments.

A leading author became involved in a sinful relationship. Confessing his errors, he also commented that, in reflection, he realized that he had no close friends to hold him accountable in his Christian lifestyle.

In the popular movie *Crocodile Dundee*, the main character, during his first visit from the wilds of Australia to New York City, is amazed by all the people who are in therapy. He had assumed that New York City would be one of the friendliest places in the world. When told that actually most New Yorkers are in counseling, he is unable to comprehend why anyone would need to pay someone to sit and listen. In shock, he exclaims, "Don't they have any mates?"

All of us need close friends with whom we can share our joys and our difficulties. We especially need some close friends whose relationships with God we respect and with whom we can be ourselves. We appreciate friends who'll laugh with us, cry with us, and pray with us. We want friends to whom we can go in times of trouble, and friends who will be willing to confront us and challenge us in areas that need it. This is difficult because most of us would rather be loved and accepted than challenged. It is out of a close relationship of love and caring with those friends of like faith and standards that the loyalty is established that allows loving confrontation.

Mothers at home with small children can be greatly helped by spending time with other mothers in the same situation. Often as we experience frustration and failure in raising young children, what we need to hear the most is someone else say, "I know exactly how you feel." Just knowing that you are not alone and that your feelings are normal will go a long way toward giving you encouragement. Our husbands cannot be expected to understand fully the challenges we face. They are not moms. We must not expect them to completely appreciate our feelings. Other mothers can fill this need and in so doing will help prevent us from putting unrealistic expectations upon our husbands.

We have a group of mothers at our church who meet every Thursday to encourage one another and to share the joys and the trials of parenting. Beth, a new mother, shared how much it helps her to see how other mothers interact with their babies. It also keeps her from feeling isolated. She is encouraged to know that some close friends in her same situation are praying for her. Often it's helpful to have a friend whose children are a bit older than yours. We look at her in amazement and wonder, "She's made it and she's still alive!" She may be a wealth of wisdom and encouragement. She will also bring some perspective to our situation and be a living reminder that this season is indeed brief.

Each of us will benefit as we seek to develop close friendships with a few other couples and families. These relationships give the children a sense of security in an "extended family" in a day when most biological families live miles apart. Knowing that your children have other adults they can go to with concerns is a great joy.

Recently, a teenage daughter of friends in another state called my husband with some problems she had in a dating relationship. Previously, we had met in a small couples' fellowship with her parents for three years. We had done many things together and with each other's children. We had been to sporting events, cooked out, and vacationed together. We had also studied the Bible and prayed together. Because of the close relationships we had developed, she felt perfectly natural in calling my husband. This meant a lot to both families.

In this busy world of fickle relationships, it's crucial to spend time with a few other couples who desire to grow in their faith and with whom you can gradually build friendships. In time these relationships will become ones in which it's natural to pray together and to encourage and to challenge one another in the priorities of family living.

In his book *For the Life of the Family*, John Yates describes how to begin a supportive parents' group. This book provides a plan of study and suggests activities for parents who will be meeting for several months. It's a good idea to include some single parents in the group. There are special times for the adults to meet with all of the children. Many people have found these small Family Life Action Groups ("FLAG" groups) tremendously helpful in building close, supportive relationships with other adults. The children benefit as well in growing closer to some of their parents' friends. These groups have the potential for developing those close relationships that we all need.[5]

Just as Jesus took time away to be with his friends Peter, James, and John, so we too need time to develop close relationships with a few friends who share a common faith in Christ. We need friends with whom we can share our successes and our failures. We need friends who will encourage us to grow in our faith. We need friends who will stick with us in the good times and the bad. God knows our needs, and as we pray for friendships like these to grow, He will bring them our way.

Our Commitment to Our Work

Our fourth priority should be our commitment to the work in the world that God has called us to do. But what exactly does that mean? If we have a profession outside the home, that is our *work*. If we stay home with our children, our *work* refers to those other people we come in contact with in our everyday lives. Perhaps it's a school committee or several neighbors or the girl at the grocery store. Commitment to our work means a commitment to people outside of our families and our churches or fellowships. These people are usually the people we meet at our place of employment or in different activities that we or our children are involved in. God has called us to go into the world and to share His love. It may be easier to spend time with Christian friends, yet then we will miss out on what God has called us to do. Our "work" is loving and serving those people with whom we have personal contact, especially reaching out to share the love of Christ with those who do not know Him. We cannot realistically love the whole world, but we can begin to love those people around us in the world in which we live.

For moms who are able to stay home with their children, there is great opportunity for reaching out to those around us. First, we must realize that God has called us to be at home during this time in our lives. Because we are at home, we will have the time to speak with people that we would not have if we worked outside the home. Second, we should ask God to give us His vision for whom He desires us especially to reach out to. Third, we must creatively think about all those people with whom we come in contact and begin to pray for them and to love them.

We all have neighbors. It is easy amid the hustle of life to go months without even seeing our neighbor. Perhaps we have a lonely neighbor who would respond with joy to some attention. Another arena young mothers find themselves in is meeting their children's friends' parents. The various school groups from preschool to PTA provide a wonderful way to reach out in love to those around us. A single parent recently met her son's friend's mother at a PTA meeting. She was lonely and looking for a church. The other girl invited her to church, and the single parent found a loving community where she came to know Christ as did her son. Four other members of her immediate family have also come to faith in Christ. Although God had long been at work, in a way the PTA meeting was a real beginning.

Sports events are another place to reach out and get to know other parents. Often it's easy just to sit with those parents we already know and miss out on the blessing of befriending someone we do not know.

All moms spend lots of time at the pediatrician's office. We should pray for our pediatricians! A couple of years ago, a new pediatrician joined a practice in our town. One mother had been praying for this group of doctors for several years. With lots of children who always seemed to be sick, she got to know this doctor quite well! She befriended the new doctor and invited her to church and to lunch. Over a period of time, she continued to reach out in friendship to this doctor. When the doctor's father became ill, she came to her friend for comfort and during this difficult time she too came to faith in Jesus Christ.

In another city, an obstetrician and his wife were befriended by a patient and her husband. They invited them to dinner and a friendship began to develop between the couples. The obstetrician and his new wife were both on their second marriages and wanted this one to be different. They were eager to learn what could make their new marriage succeed. As the patient and her husband shared the message of Christ, their new friends expressed a desire to learn more. In time, this doctor and his wife came to know Christ in a personal way and their marriage has indeed benefited.

We are all surrounded by people. From the grocery store clerks, to school teachers, to our postman, God has called us to be reaching out in love to those in our world.

One of the special blessings of being at home with our children is having the luxury of reaching out together. Perhaps it will be inviting a newcomer and her child over to play, then inviting them to church. Praying with our children about those for whom God would have us care gives us a wonderful opportunity to teach our children, from an early age, to love others. It gives us the blessing of ministering together and together seeing God answer our prayers. Recently a five-year-old little girl talked to her best friend at school about the love of Christ. Her family began to pray for and to reach out to this other family. Soon the whole family came to know Christ through their own daughter's new faith which had been shared with her by her schoolmate.

As mothers at home, we have the challenge to think of all the different people with whom we come in contact. When we begin to pray for them and to care for them with our families, we will experience the joy of seeing God use us and our children to bring others to experience His love. In the process, our whole families will be blessed.

For mothers who work outside the home, the same principles apply. Begin to ask God to show you the people He has for you to care for. It may be a co-worker, a secretary, the one who cleans the office, or your employer. Take an interest in them personally. Share a lunch or "break" with them. Pray and ask God how you can help others in your office come to know and experience His love. If there is another believer where you work, you might want to meet to talk about how you can together reach out to those around you.

My friend Grace recently returned to teaching in a local public high school. She prayed that God would help her make a difference for good in the school. God has answered Grace's prayer. She has begun a fellowship group before school one morning each week where other faculty and staff who desire to can come together to pray and encourage each other in their roles in the school. This fellowship group has been a wonderful blessing to those involved. Hearing about Grace's group, another teacher in a nearby school hopes to begin one for her co-workers.

Whether we work outside the home or spend this season at home, God has called us to be the light of the world in order that others might come to know Him (see Matthew 5:14-16). He desires for us to act like His children no matter where we are or whom we are with. Our character and behavior should be the same in all places. We don't have one personality for church meetings, another for work, and another for being at home. We are called to be His children wherever we are. In whatever place God has called us to be, we should be asking Him for help in bringing His love to those around us.

Relating the Priorities Together

Our commitment to Christ, commitment to our families, commitment to a group of close friends, and our commitment to our work are the four priorities that Biblical teaching seems to confirm. These priorities enable us to know who we are and how we should live in this busy world. When we keep these priorities generally in this order, we will experience meaning and balance in our lives. A sense of purpose will be produced as the priorities enable us to determine our schedules rather than having our schedules run us. When we feel out of control and overwhelmed, it is helpful to step back and have a "priority check" to determine if one priority has somehow been slighted or misplaced.

Perhaps I have a real case of the "spiritual blues." My faith is not exciting. I'm bored, frustrated, and restless in my situation. When this has been true in my own life and I've run a "priority check," I've often found that I've neglected to spend time alone with God. My quiet times have fallen away. I need to take time to be alone with God and with the psalmist pray, "Restore unto me the joy of thy salvation and sustain me with a willing spirit" (Psalm 51:12). As I again spend time in His Word and with God, I find that He rejuvenates me. He is always glad to have me "back." It is amazing that our Heavenly Father loves us continually and that He longs to spend time alone with us.

At another time we may find ourselves "stuck in a rut," always seeing the same people and not feeling like we are growing or reaching out. Perhaps the fourth priority of our commitment to work in the world has dropped from sight. We ought to come to God asking for a fresh vision for whom He would desire us to care for.

On the other hand, we may be trying to grow as a Christian by ourselves. We may feel lonely and frustrated. Where are those close friends we need? Possibly we need to find a small group of other women that we can meet with to grow together. Often being around other women who are excited about studying the Bible and praying will encourage us when we are not inclined to do so by ourselves.

Whatever the cause of "spiritual blues," running a priority check can be helpful in pointing us toward some positive steps to take to help restore us to a sense of purpose and peace. Of necessity there will be seasons in which one priority will overrule all others: tax season for accountants, the birth of a child, beginning a business, and the like. The challenge is to keep these four priorities as a basis for determining how we want to live. If we are always at spiritual meetings, Bible studies, church, and the like, and never at a soccer game, our children will grow up resenting the church. If we are spending more and more time with our children and neglecting our marriages, we'll find we don't have much of a marriage left when the children leave. If we spend every moment at the office and neglect the family, we may find ourselves in the same boat as the dad in "Cat's in the Cradle." That dad never had time to spend with his son, then he was saddened when he was an old man and his grown son was too busy to spend time with him.

Our children need priorities to live by as well, and they will learn them from us whether we like it or not. For example, the parents who drop their children off at church and return home to read Sunday's paper are communicating that church is a priority for children but not for adults. When the children become adolescents, church will become unimportant for them—it's "kid stuff." Our lives speak loudly in showing our children what we think is important and what is not. We often fail in living up to our priorities, but it is important that we talk with our children about what is important to us and the ways in which we are trying to live out these priorities.

It is a great challenge to discuss these priorities around the table as the kids grow and to get their ideas as to how we can work on them as individuals and families. Many times they have insights and observations that we haven't thought of or perhaps that we don't want to hear. When it is appropriate, we must be honest with our children about our own struggles and listen to their input, trying to implement any worthwhile suggestions they may have.

Priorities are meant to be guidelines to freedom much as learning how to utilize the rudder in sailing opens up seas to the explorer. If we have no priorities, we are like the ship without a rudder. Without priorities we will find ourselves being overwhelmed by the numerous choices around us, and we will become responders to the world's demands rather than determiners of our lives.

Priorities based on the principles in God's Word are the best basis for living because He created us, and He knows what is right for us. As we creatively implement God's priorities in our lives, we will experience a security in knowing who we are and what we're about, and our children will have this same sense of security.

Focus Questions

Meditate on Christ's prayer in John 17.

1. How do I see the priorities illustrated in this prayer?
2. What do I learn about my own prayer life from Jesus' prayer?
3. Which priority in my life needs work during this "season"?
4. What steps shall I take this week to live out my priorities?

Meditate on Psalm 119:33-40, making it a personal prayer.

FIVE

BECOMING A BEST FRIEND IN MARRIAGE

"Cameras rolling, background, action."

Slowly I walked down the steps of the Lincoln Memorial, gazing across the vast white marble that seemed to stretch forever. It was the twentieth take of one, two-minute scene in a made-for-television movie. My part was that of a business executive walking past the leading characters.

The weather was surprisingly cold for late fall in Washington, D.C. Throughout the day, I huddled along with the other actors and actresses just to keep warm. We got to know each other quite well in the process. They were a seemingly happy lot, and one fellow, Steve, soon emerged as the group clown. He kept everyone laughing with tales of his sexual exploits and dirty jokes. Not one of the other twelve actresses and actors was married. Several had been married at least once, but most were just involved in living with their current mate.

During a rare lull in the boisterous conversations, one of the other girls asked me, "Susan, what about you? Have you got a boyfriend?"

"I sure do," I replied. "I've been married for seventeen years, and my husband is wonderful."

There was an audible silence as a shocked look crossed Steve's face. "I've never met anyone before who has been married that long and is happy," he responded in amazement. "How do you do it?"

There was no way to answer Steve briefly; indeed, we talked for many hours, yet the essence of my response can be summarized quite simply: "Steve, my husband and I made a commit-

ment to the permanence of the marriage. We put Jesus Christ at
the center of the relationship, and we work hard at becoming each
other's best friend."

It is easy to make a statement like that. It is a lot harder to
implement it! It is especially hard for young mothers with several
small children to have the time, the energy, and the discipline to
work at cultivating their friendships with their husbands.

It is often the first ten to fifteen years of a marriage that are
crucial in laying the foundation for a solid, happy relationship.
Building an intimate friendship with your mate is pivotal to that
healthy relationship, yet it is in these early years that many couples have the most stress put on their marriage—stresses that will
tend to unravel the friendship rather than deepen it.

During these years the wife is overwhelmed with small children. It is also likely to be a crucial time in the husband's career.
Perhaps he's starting his own business or is on the fast track in his
profession. He is under tremendous pressure. It may be a time of
financial difficulty as well. The living space gets smaller as the
family begins to grow. Moving to another home may be a big
step. Perhaps one of the mates is having to deal with an ill or
aging parent.

All in all, it's a season of stress. Stress from small children,
stress from career, stress from extended family, and added to these
are the stresses inherent in the normal adjustments of marriage.
Usually, we enter into marriage with a solid growing friendship
with our mates, but then as this blanket of tension surrounds us,
we find ourselves just trying to get through each day. We scarcely
realize that our tendency is to deal with the stresses individually
rather than responding together.

Overcoming Our Tendency Toward Separateness

Throughout all time, little girls have looked to marriage as the
culmination of all of one's hopes and dreams. From ancient fairy
tales to contemporary media, a happy marriage is idolized as a
final ideal. Even with staggering divorce statistics and couples
choosing to live together outside of marriage, the ideal remains.
When you marry, you may feel you have in a sense arrived. Marriage is often viewed as the culmination rather than the begin-

ning. Herein lies the problem. In reality, when we say, "I do," we are committing ourselves anew to work at the relationship.

One of the first things we have to work on is our tendency toward separateness. Living alone for years we naturally establish independent ways. We have the luxury of considering our own needs and not the needs of a partner. Then we get married and as Genesis 2:24 says, "For this cause a man shall leave his father and his mother, and shall cleave to his wife; and they shall become one flesh."

This can be a shock to the system. Becoming one in a total sense does not happen overnight. Two people with different backgrounds, different experiences, and unique personalities do not become one (other than physically) in a brief time. It takes a lifetime. We must get a lifetime perspective in our marriages. It will take a lifetime of work to overcome our tendency toward separateness and to learn the joys of oneness that God has intended the marriage to illustrate. A commitment to the permanence of marriage is also crucial in overcoming our separateness. When we decide from the beginning that divorce is not an option, then we will strive to work out our problems. Once married, we can no longer have the mentality of the high school student who said, "Well, if he doesn't do such and such, I just won't speak to him again." When we are committed to living with our mates forever, we know we can't withdraw emotionally because that makes the marriage unbearable.

So it is essential to set aside an appropriate time to discuss the difficulties in the relationship. As we attack the problems in our marriages together rather than attacking each other, our relationships will be deepened by a joint approach to the normal conflicts inherent in every marriage.

I remember a big argument early in our marriage. In a fit of tears I said to Johnny, "Well, maybe we should never have gotten married in the first place."

He looked at me and with unusually fierce conviction said, "Don't you ever say that again." His message was quite clear, and I've never said that again.

My friend Holly tells of an early fight with her husband Jerry. Sobbing hysterically over a misunderstanding in their relationship, she locked herself in the bathroom. As she cried out, "I just want to die," Jerry pounded on the bathroom door.

"Open the door, Holly, or I'll bash it down."

Now Jerry is a big football player who could easily have done just that, so Holly opened the door. Jerry entered with a piece of paper in his hands. On the paper he had drawn a line across the entire length of the page. In the center of the line he had placed a tiny dot.

"Holly," he said, "this line is our marriage. It goes on and on. The tiny dot is this one fight. It is small, and it ends, but our marriage survives."

We cannot entertain the idea of escape in our marriages (although, if abuse is going on, that must be dealt with). Instead we should view our marriage commitment as permanent, and with that security no longer in question, we will find that we will make a greater effort in building the marriage friendship.

Marriage therapist Dr. David Fenell recently completed a study of one hundred fifty couples, all of whom had been married more than twenty years. According to his study, he found that "a commitment to the institution of marriage" topped the list of essential characteristics that enabled a marriage to last for decades. Second in his findings was a "commitment to the marriage partner."[1]

Viewing marriage as a life-long commitment should bring great freedom and joy. Picture the commitment as an impenetrable, protective fence around the relationship. The fence offers security and protection. It enables those inside to have a feeling of belonging. The sense of protection supplied by this fence of commitment enables the partners to grow as best friends working through problems as they come up, yet without fear. The security of the commitment allows for failure. It encourages growth, and it allows for hope.

As we have the mindset of a permanent commitment in our marriages, we have an imperfect mirror image of God's commitment to us. His commitment to us is absolutely permanent. He will never leave us or forsake us (Hebrews 13:5). His love is perfect. In marriage, we are given a small glimpse of His everlasting commitment to us.

Another element in learning how to overcome our tendency

toward separateness involves the way we deal with the problems that arise in a marriage. When faced with a problem between spouses, we either overlook it, deny it, or deal with it. Sometimes we will overlook a problem because it's just not important enough to make an issue of. On the other hand, it may be important, but the process of dealing with the issue is too painful for us so we withdraw into our "separateness," unwilling to go through the pain of an unpleasant scene with our mate.

A close friend of mine recently separated from her husband. When I asked her where things started to go wrong, she said, "Whenever I would try to discuss problems in our marriage that would be hurtful to discuss or painful to deal with, he would not want to discuss them. He simply did not want to deal with painful things, so we never did, and we began to grow apart."

Growing, of necessity, involves suffering and hurt. It cannot be avoided because marriage always involves two self-centered people whose natural instincts are to please themselves. Peeling away these layers of ourselves involves pain, but the joy that occurs as we see the merging of two is far greater than the pain. When pain and suffering come, it is essential that we must fix our eyes on Christ. If we are willing to walk through the pain giving more of ourselves away, God's loving result will be a growing oneness with our mates.

Occasionally, we will deny there is a problem. Perhaps we deny the existence of a problem out of fear—fear that the problem cannot be overcome. We see this in homes where there is alcoholism. We may fear that we can't change or they can't change. Or possibly we don't want to change so we rationalize away the problem. We withdraw into our separate worlds ignoring a growing and potentially devastating illness.

In some cases, our mates may feel there is a problem when we don't. We cannot dismiss this, as much as we'd like to, because if we are to be best friends—to build real oneness in marriage— what is a problem to one is a problem to both and needs to be worked out.

The difficulties we will face are not unique. Other couples have faced the same ones. As we confront these challenges, God has promised to provide answers. He will show us a way out (see 1 Corinthians 10:13). Facing our problems will, in the long run, lead to a deeper friendship in our marriage. As children, we had to learn to face our difficulties and to overcome them. We have to carry this over into our marriages.

I remember teaching the twins to ride their two-wheel bikes. Susy caught on rather quickly. Her bike was a bit smaller than Libby's, and it was easier for her to control. Susy was soon biking away while Libby sat in the middle of the street beside a fallen bike in a fit of tears. Frustration and agony were written all over her little face as she said to me, "Mom, I just can't do it. I hate bikes."

"Sure you can," I replied.

"No, I can't, and I don't ever want to," sobbed Libby.

Days later after hours of coaching and encouraging words from many family members, Libby began, wobbly at first, to pedal all alone. Her face broke into a huge smile, and I'm sure my whole neighborhood heard her screaming, "I can do it, I can do it!"

Soon she began to fly, and the joy she felt was such a contrast to the defeat she had experienced only a few days earlier. She had faced her problem and by being encouraged and by not being allowed to give up, she had worked and conquered the challenge. The joy in victory soon caused her to forget most of her pain in learning, and to this day, she appreciates her bike more than her twin who had an easier time learning. As we face challenges in our marriages and work through them, we will experience incredible joy and victory when we come out on the other side. To grow as best friends means to deny the tendency to withdraw when we are faced with problems and to begin to face them together, seeing the problems as opportunities for God to peel back the layers of separateness and to continue to mold us into a partnership of best friends.

Dear Steve:

When we worked on the film, you asked how a relationship lasted. The commitment to "til death do us part" is a wonderful blessing. It provides the security and the protection for the pains and the joys that take place in growing a friendship in marriage. It gives us the hope of a relationship that will last in a world of broken promises.

Changing Expectations

As we grow in overcoming our tendency toward separateness, we will also discover that our expectations in marriage are changing. Just as our expectations of ourselves as women, wives, and mothers come in part from the families in which we grew up, our expectations of marriage come in part from our parents' marriages. The closest model we have had of a marriage is our parents' marriages. Many of the expectations we have of our husbands will be influenced by our fathers.

R.C. Sproul once said that "if you imagined your mother married to your father-in-law, and your father married to your mother-in-law, you'd have a good picture of the dynamics of your marriage." I grew up in a home where my dad was a "Mr. Fix-it." When anything broke, he fixed it. Johnny grew up in a home where his dad wasn't interested in fixing things. It was his mother's job to call the repairman. One of our first misunderstandings as newlyweds was when an appliance broke. I kept hinting for Johnny to fix it, but to no avail. Finally in a fit of exasperation, I said, "Why haven't you fixed it?"

He responded, "Why haven't you called the repairman?" I must admit that in years since, he has become a better Mr. Fix-it, and I have called in a repairman a few times as well!

A friend of mine grew up with a father who was very difficult to please. He was impatient, intolerant, and very critical of her. She vowed she would never marry a man like her dad. When she married a wonderful man, she found that if he was ever the least bit critical, she would overreact and blow up. It took some time for her to realize that she was expecting her husband to behave like her dad, and this was damaging to their relationship. In fact, her husband was not at all like her dad. Once she realized what was happening, she and her husband were able to discuss it and ask God to change her perspective and heal her wounds. Her own home life had programmed her to have unfair expectations of her husband.

In coming from different homes, we bring differing expectations into marriage. As we develop our own sense of family, each of us will have expectations that need to be changed. As we grow in creating our own concept of family, we will begin to build similar expectations unique to our own relationship. But first we must eliminate unfair expectations.

A common expectation that often causes trouble in a marriage is the expectation that my mate will meet my needs. The young mother suffering from a loss of self-worth will often find herself looking to her husband to meet her emotional needs and make her feel worthwhile. It might happen like this.

After a long day of running errands which means strapping seatbelts endless times, putting on coats and hats over and over, and saying "no" to the "I wants" at the grocery store, and finally arriving home just as the baby falls asleep in the car seat, the wife is exhausted! She makes a dash to pick up things around the house and get dinner on the table all while the now wide-awake baby screams. The wife anxiously awaits her husband's arrival and his appreciation of her hard work.

In he comes after a brutal day where nothing he did could please his boss. He gives her the customary kiss hello and collapses into the nearest chair while she is left to get the children into bed. Worried about his work situation, he fails to notice his wife's silence. He needs to be affirmed. She needs to be appreciated. Both are expecting the other person to meet their needs. Because the partners are too tired to talk, they go to bed let down because their mate failed to meet their expectations.

Although becoming best friends involves communicating about our needs and attempting to help meet each other's needs, ultimately we must realize that our mates can never meet *all* of our emotional needs. Too often wives place unrealistic expectations upon their husbands to meet needs that God alone or others can meet. It is unfair to put the burden of our emotional well-being on our husbands alone. We must look to God first for approval, for understanding, and for empathy. When we experience disappointment from our husband's lack of response to us in different areas, we should ask ourselves the question, "Am I expecting my husband to meet this particular need in my life when I should be looking to God to do it?"

Not only does God know both me and my husband totally, He loves each of us completely. Oh, to be known completely and loved totally is almost too good to be true, and seems impossible to believe, yet that is exactly how God feels about us. He knows that I need to seek Him first (see Matthew 6:33), for apart from His help, I cannot be the wife I want to be. He alone knows all of my needs, and He alone can fulfill these needs. He also knows my husband's needs. As I turn to Him for help, I am going to the source of all knowledge and all power. He desires for me to come to Him asking, "Lord, help me to come to you with my needs. Help me to recognize my husband's needs and show me how I can help meet them in my role as his wife and best friend."

Our expectation in marriage should be that as we individually grow in our relationship with Christ we will learn more and more how to meet each other's needs as best friends.

Part of learning to deal with unrealistic expectations involves recognizing the differences in sexes. Women generally are more aware of their feelings than men. Usually, they feel a greater recognized need for intimacy. Romance is more important to the typical wife than to the husband. She wants hugs, kisses, and communication, while he is more anxious to jump into bed. Much has been written about these distinctions, but it's helpful to keep them in mind when discussing expectations.

We need to understand the differences between the sexes rather than resent them. It's all too easy to resent the fact that my husband doesn't handle me the way he should when it's so obvious to me how easy it would be to make me happy. It is indeed obvious to our female eyes, but it can be foreign to his.

A friend of mine who has been married three months called this week. She was mad with her husband because she had worked hard and lost five pounds. She dressed nicely for work in a skirt that used to be a bit snug but now fit loosely. She expected her husband to notice her weight loss and compliment her on how good she looked. By evening when he had not made one comment on her appearance, she was devastated. First she was hurt, then she was mad all because the poor man had not met her expectation of noticing and complimenting her on her appearance.

She expected him to respond the way she would, and in the newness of marriage she was beginning to learn that men are different, and it's unfair of us to demand that they be like us. Thank heavens they are not! No matter what the latest cultural theory teaches about sexuality, God has spoken in His Word, "male and female He created them" (Genesis 1:27).

Not only do our differences as male and female play a part in our expectations, but also our different expectations in roles as wife and husband need to be addressed. From an emphasis on "submission" of the wife to the cry for women's "liberation," there has been confusion in Christian circles as to the roles and behavior of mates. On the one hand, damage in some marriages has been caused by the overly "submissive" wife. Believing herself to be fulfilling God's role for her, she sublimates her own opinions and desires in an effort to please her husband. Years pass and in her quiet acquiescence to her husband's leadership, she neglects to use her own gifts and insights. Bitterness grows and finally there is an explosion as her spirit snaps in confrontation and anger with her husband. He is amazed at this "sudden" personality change. Because of years of submerging her true self under her husband, there has not been a true growing oneness in the marriage, and the marriage is in trouble.

Another possibility might be that instead of bitterness, acquiescence gives way to resignation, and the wife becomes dull and resigned. In both situations the partners can become vulnerable to attentions from other members of the opposite sex.

On the other hand, the "liberated" wife, in an attempt to make sure that her husband recognizes her equality, becomes more dominant and more aggressive, supplanting him as the leader in the relationship. As she senses the subtle change and her ability to control him, slowly her respect for him as a man diminishes. When a woman loses respect for her husband, the marriage is in trouble. She, perhaps unknowingly, will begin to look to men she does respect, and temptations will follow.

Both of these are extreme and neither is right. In both situations healing is possible. But often the healing will need the gentle guidance of a godly counselor because personalities of the mates must be restored before the rebuilding of oneness can be seen. *It is so important to get help when it is needed.* There is much good help available, and it's crucial that pride be swallowed and help sought. A marriage is too precious not to salvage.

Marriage roles are always changing and mutual respect is crucial. God's roles withstand cultural fads. God has called us to be "subject to one another in the fear of Christ" (Ephesians 5:21). Our submission is first to the Lord. As we seek to obey Him, we will *both* submit to one another. We are called to be partners—to be one. In Galatians 3:28 we read, "There is neither male nor female; for you are all one in Christ Jesus." We are to "do nothing from selfishness or empty conceit, but with humility of mind let each of you regard one another as more important than himself" (Philippians 2:3).

Scripture teaches that God intends for the husband to be the head of the family (see Ephesians 5:23), yet when both partners are seeking to serve one another, the issue of submission and leadership becomes practically irrelevant. It becomes a nonissue when we each seek to follow God first and sacrificially serve each other.

We will have different expectations in marriage because of our sex and because of our different concepts of marital roles. We'll also have different expectations because we're different people with unique natures.

Part of the initial attraction that draws couples together has to do with common interests. We like to be with someone who enjoys the same things we do. Congeniality grows as two people spend time pursuing the same interests. While we are often drawn to marriage by common interests, we fail to realize the differences in our nature until we are married.

Often the qualities in our mates that originally attracted us are those same qualities that can prove frustrating in marriage. I was always attracted to Johnny because he had a stable sense about him. I trusted his judgment. I knew he was totally responsible, and he would never do anything "weird." He was very even-tempered. He was to me, in a sense, a rock.

I, on the other hand, was more creative, romantic, impulsive, and cause-oriented. His stability gave me real freedom. In a marriage, these initial attractions can become irritants. I often wished my husband would not be quite so predictable, would do something terribly romantic, or would buy me a surprise gift—not one I'd picked out for him to give me!

We have to recognize differences in our mates and turn them into blessings. We can't expect our mates to be like us or even like our fathers. We must allow each other to be different, then work together through communicating how our differences in nature can actually strengthen our marriages.

Another difference we've noticed in our marriage is that I am a visionary. It is easy for me to see a need in the world and come up with many ideas as to how to meet that need or solve that particular problem. When we were first married, this was a threat to my husband. He felt that since he was the one who was a minister, he should be the one with the plans. However, when he realized that God had given me that gift to complement his gifts, he was able to appreciate the differences in our gifts. Often my dreams and ideas are totally inappropriate, and he has the insight to be able to determine what is right to implement and what is not. I don't have this sense of objective wisdom. God has given each of us unique gifts.

As unique individuals we have special gifts that our mates need. Our husbands have special gifts that we need. Part of the fun of growing in a marriage is discovering and continuing to perfect these gifts. Building a best friendship is learning how to encourage each other's gifts—not seeing them as threats but as complements to the marriage partner. Our mate must be our friend, not our enemy. He is not my competition. He's on my team!

In a sense the way the larger body of Christ works best is seen in microcosm in marriage. There are gifts which only I can supply in our marriage, and there are gifts or talents which only my husband can supply. As we bring these gifts into marriage, the result will be the building up of the "marriage" in love (see Ephesians 4:16).

One of the pleasures in marriage is the expectation of having years ahead to enjoy discovering our own gifts and those of our husbands and to see how we unite to reflect the body of Christ. We cannot discover our own gifts apart from interaction with other people. God has not created us to be solitary beings. In giving us mates, He has given us a treasure that will help us come to know who we ourselves are.

For several summers my boys have been invited to the beach with a dear older couple in our church. My boys love this special time with Al and Jean. One of the favorite attractions is the giant jigsaw puzzles that they work on. The puzzles have many different pieces. Each piece is cut differently with as many different colors as possible to frustrate the worker! When the pieces are spread out alone on the card table, it is difficult to see how they relate to each other or to see any beauty in "separateness." However, as the pieces begin to fit together and the puzzles give hints of a beautiful picture, there is excitement and satisfaction on the part of the boys. So it is in our marriages. When we grow with one another in marriage, we will discover our unique gifts. As we continually learn how to fit these gifts together piece by piece in harmony, we will experience the joy and satisfaction in marital oneness that Christ intended.

Not only do we have unique natures with special gifts to bring into the marriage, we also come into marriage full of weaknesses. Alas, the expectations of matrimony did not include having to learn how to live with the weaknesses of my mate! Sometimes our gifts can become our weaknesses. For example, a creative person usually has a vivid imagination. This is wonderful until that person gets the flu, and immediately is sure she's dying of leukemia. Or your child has a headache, and you're sure it's a brain tumor. It is maddening, and yet it's a weakness that we must recognize and give to God. Take heart, we are in good company! When the Apostle Paul was struggling with his weaknesses, God spoke to him and said, "My grace is sufficient for you, for power is perfected in weakness" (2 Corinthians 12:9). It is in our weaknesses that we come to know God's love and power the most. It is helpful to see weaknesses as the negative side of a gift and to ask what is the gift and how can it be encouraged.

As we notice weakness in our mates, we should ask, "How can my gifts fill that weakness in my husband?" I am more sensitive by nature. Sometimes my husband is not as sensitive to people as he should be. Their feelings get hurt. So when I sense that a friend is in need of some special attention from my husband, I clue him in. On the other hand, if I overreact to a situation or to a person, Johnny is able to be more objective and to encourage me to relax. His gift covers my weakness. Noticing these differences in nature and seeing how they can work together within the marriage is a part of building a best friendship.

While we can often use our gifts to balance our husband's weaknesses we must take care that we do not attempt to change his weaknesses into strengths. There's a tremendous temptation for us to try to play God in another's life. This will lead only to bitterness and resentment on the part of the mate. We have to learn to practice acceptance with our mates, particularly in the area of what we consider "weakness."

I have a friend whose husband is very shy. She is tremendously outgoing and loves to be with people. He is so reserved that being with a group of people is actually agony for him. Early in their marriage this was very difficult for her since she wanted him to be more outgoing. She wanted him to be like herself, and she resented this "weakness" in his personality.

She is a godly woman committed to her marriage and very much in love with her husband. As she's faced this problem and worked through it, she has seen that she must accept him as he is and learn to use her outgoing nature to complement his shyness. She's also learned that he has great gifts of wisdom and perception that his quiet nature and powers of observation have cultivated. She needs these gifts to complete her. It has not been easy, and both mates have made sacrifices. She has given up events she would have liked to attend, and he's gone to some when he'd rather have stayed home. Yet they are experiencing the joy of seeing how their different natures with weaknesses and strengths can be meshed together when they learn to accept one another just as they are.

As we grow in acquiring realistic expectations, it's important to continually allow our mates room to grow and room to change. It can be frustrating for the mate when the spouse expects the same behavior and response always. That stifles growth. Particularly as we go to God with our weaknesses and begin to see Him work in new areas of our lives, we need to see our mates expressing belief in us. We should have expectations of change in each other. We need to believe the good in our mates.

Dear Steve:

Part of "making it" in marriage is realizing that alone you can't "make it"! The answer lies in being able to look to God who made me and my mate and who knows and loves us. He alone knows all of our gifts and all of our weaknesses. As we look to Him, He will gently lead each of us into a deeper awareness of how to meet each other's needs. God is the creator of marriage. He is the sustainer and builder as well. He is the one who will turn two different people into a miracle of oneness—where there is unity alongside diversity.

Growing in Communication

I don't think that I've ever heard a talk on marriage that did not deal with the problem of communication. Not only does the problem of communication crop up in marriage seminars, it is evident in every facet of the work world. Clear communication is crucial in every growing relationship.

The president of the country needs to have good communication with his aides if he is to be effective. Businessmen need to have good communication with their sales and production staffs if they are to achieve profitability. Husbands and wives need good communication with each other if their marriage is to be continually deepening in friendship. We all know the importance of communication, yet the challenge of not just maintaining clear communication but growing deeper in communication is often difficult in marriage. Our intentions are good; we want good communication, yet in this busy season, it's not so easy to get it!

We are surrounded by small children. Our husbands' careers and possibly ours are demanding. The community needs us. The church needs us. We are exhausted trying to fit it all in, and by the time we actually see each other, we're too tired to talk. The biggest complaint of wives who are dealing with several small children is that they don't have enough meaningful communication with their husbands. Perhaps the wife has been coping with small children all day, cooing at the baby, reading Dr. Seuss, giving simple answers to silly questions. She's practically forgotten how to use a compound sentence or think about complex issues. She longs for some adult conversation and intimate sharing with her husband.

He, however, has had an intense day of relating to other adults, and when he arrives home the last thing he wants to do is talk. In a household with lots of children, it is difficult to have meaningful communication anyway. There are children to be fed, bathed, and put to bed. Communication between partners becomes functional at best. There are phone calls to answer, arrangements to be made. Who is going to get the car inspected?

Whom shall we have to the dinner party? Was the laundry picked up? Oh, and did you remember to call your mother? At last the mates drop into bed exhausted and fall asleep only to awake to another day of mundane noncommunication.

As busy parents we all find ourselves in this vicious cycle, and yet the danger is that we accept it as inevitable, thinking, *This is as good as it can be at this stage*. We don't make the effort to grow in deepening the communication and moving from pure functional communication to the sharing of our very hearts and souls.

It is most often the wife who will recognize the need for deeper communication. We must help our husbands see this need, then think together as to how we can grow deeper in communicating. First we must avoid the tendency to blame our husbands. "He won't talk to me," is a common cry. "Our schedules are too busy." Or, "His work is more important than his family."

Blaming our husbands for a lack of communication in busy marriages with young children is not fair. It's not his fault. It's the season we're in, and it's our problem together. The first step is to recognize the normalcy of the problem and not place blame. We must realize this problem is universal, but we do *not* have to accept it as something we must live with. God wants us to be growing in our communication, and there are many ways this can happen, even in busy households full of small children.

So first, it is necessary to avoid placing blame and second, we must refuse to accept mere functional communication as the norm. Instead, we must determine to work for a deeper level of sharing. As we work toward a deepening communication in our marriages, several things will become evident. Creating the right place and the right time for talking can be a challenge in busy households. Often in our eagerness to talk to another adult, we might hit our husbands over the head with urgent items when they first come in the front door. It may be wiser to let them unwind first. On the other hand, schedules may not allow for indepth communication before he heads back out the door to an evening meeting. This was true in our marriage.

When our children were three/three, six, eight, and ten, I realized that when Johnny arrived home after a long day, the children all had different things they wanted their dad to do with them. One wanted to play baseball, one wanted to color, and the like. From the moment he hit the door until supper, he was a kid again. This was great, except that he has many evening meetings and immediately after supper he was off again, and *we'd hardly gotten to visit.*

Unfortunately, our conversation dwindled to the functional. We decided that the children needed to know that though dad loved them immensely, our relationship as husband and wife was priority. So in the evenings when he arrived, we established a "tea talk." Mom and dad would get to have the first fifteen minutes just to share with each other over a cup of tea. The children were allowed to be with us, but not speak. They soon became bored. It's been wonderful for us, and the children are learning subconsciously that mates must work at taking time to communicate.

Hopefully, they will remember this in their own marriages! A few weeks after we began this, the twins asked for their thermoses in the tub. When I asked, "What do you want your thermoses for?" One replied, "We're going to have our tea talk in the bathtub."

Everyone's marriage is different, and we need to think through the distinctions in our marriage before deciding the best time for regular communications. We all want times for easy care-free communication where we open ourselves in joy to one another. Not only are time and place important in communication, but having the right *kind* of communication is crucial. Sometimes in marriage, frustrations arise because we have become so used to communicating purely about functional things that we actually forget how to go deeper. We look at our spouse and can't think of anything to say.

When Johnny and I began our tea talks, we'd take turns sharing not only about the events of our day, but also how we *felt* about them. We'd talk about how we *felt* about ourselves. Johnny's initial response was, "I don't think about how I feel. I don't have that many feelings. I just do my work." However, as we began to talk further, feelings did begin to surface, and we began to talk on a deeper level. It can be awkward at first, yet growth is by nature awkward. Generally women are more aware of the need for deeper communication. *Men need it; they just don't realize it.* We have to help them grow into deeper sharing, taking care not to blame them when they don't see things as we do.

It is important to be especially careful when a problem or a misunderstanding needs to be discussed. My husband is not a night person; he prefers morning. After ten o'clock at night, he's not the best person to try to have a deep conversation with. I discovered that if we saved up our disagreements to discuss late at night, we often said things we wished we had not. We were too tired to discuss a sensitive issue. It is not wise to discuss sensitive issues when mates are tired. It is also not wise to discuss a sensitive issue when your spouse's emotional plate is full. If there is an overwhelming burden on our spouses because of tensions at work or a project due, it is best to wait to discuss something.

There are other times when we need to get misunderstandings straight immediately. Waiting in these cases will only allow for bitterness to fester. When a mate has been wronged, we need to deal with it immediately and ask forgiveness. Perhaps the mate may not even know they have hurt their partner. It is up to the injured one gently to tell their mate how she/he has been hurt.

Often a wife will see needs clearly. An example might be one Saturday morning. While hubby is curled up reading the paper, mom is dealing with the same endless chores she does every morning. She wishes her mate would offer to help, and she waits for him to see he is needed. He doesn't, and she becomes angry. He knows she's mad at him but he hasn't a *clue* as to what he has done. She has unconsciously put him in the position of having to guess what's on her mind, and this is unfair.

The conflict could have been avoided had the wife said, "Honey, it's Saturday, and I know you need to relax. I'm tired, too. There are several things that must be done. Would you take on a couple and I'll do the others?" Our needs vary according to our situations, but the important thing is not to expect our husband to be a mind reader.

Humor plays a much-needed role in marriage. So often a good laugh or a joke diffuses tension. We all take ourselves too seriously, and we must learn to laugh at ourselves and at our problems. Sometimes when we are in the midst of a difficult situation, it helps to mentally step back and think how funny this would look to someone who had been married fifty years. Gaining some perspective on our situations and laughing at ourselves will greatly aid in communication.

Once in a while there may be a very difficult tension in the marriage—the "sore subject." When this topic is mentioned, conflict appears instantly. We know we ought to face this problem, yet whenever we do, we seem to argue and not get anywhere. How can we deal with the "sore subject"?

One approach is to write a note to our spouses relating our thoughts about the "sore subject." When we put our thoughts in writing we will avoid the emotional fireworks that come through in verbal communication. Writing things down also gives our mates time to think about things and not have to respond immediately. Occasionally, it helps to set up a time several days away to discuss how we can come to agreement on handling the "sore subject." In our careers we set up times to discuss how to handle thorny problems, yet we often fail to do this in our marriages. As we meet to discuss the "sore subject," we should keep several things in mind.

Before beginning our discussion, we should pray together asking for God's leading in the conversation. The most precious and the most powerful form of communication with our mates occurs when we pray together. God has promised to hear our prayers and to answer them (see 1 John 5:14, Matthew 18:19). As we go to God together, we are reminded that His power holds our marriages together. Praying together also has a wonderful way of dissolving tensions. It enables us together to seek God's wisdom about family decisions.

Our relationship is more important than the "sore subject," so as we talk we must attack the problem rather than each other. We must be willing to give all of our rights away, to sacrifice, to hurt, and to work for the sake of the relationship. Sometimes we may have to ask forgiveness of our mate. Perhaps we must forgive them. In every marriage mates must go to each other confessing their sins, seeking forgiveness, and being forgiven. We will not always feel like doing it, but we must if the marriage is to grow. We should take care to listen to our mate. We should attempt to brainstorm creatively together as to every conceivable possible solution to the situation. It is helpful to ask, "What is the best solution for the sake of the whole family?"

Finally we can have a vision that through working together towards a solution to the "sore subject" we will actually have the opportunity to be molded individually, closer to Christ and closer to each other. God allows problems in our relationships. He desires for us to see them as instruments to lead us closer to Himself and closer to each other.

Communication is a challenge in every marriage. Whether we are discussing a "sore subject," or simply talking about the events of the day, there is a longing on the part of both mates to be understood. God is the only one who understands both of us. Talking to God together brings us into the presence of the One who created marriage and who knows how we will best fit together. Prayer is thus, in a sense, the soul of the marriage.

Praying together on a regular basis will bring a new dimension to the friendship. In beginning to pray, it is helpful if you share one concern about anything—a child, a neighbor—which you have with your spouse, then have him share one with you like a job project or an employee need. Simply pray for each other's concern. You might also pray the Lord's prayer together. As we pray together, we'll grow closer to God and to one another.

Dear Steve:

One of the greatest joys in a lasting relationship is learning how to communicate at a deeper level. There is no greater joy than having the one you love more than anyone in the whole world open himself/herself to you to be known by you and to know you in return. This sense of belonging is what being a best friend is all about.

Taking Time to Grow

The single greatest stress upon young couples involves finding a way to spend meaningful time together as couples. We live in a time of widespread opportunities and taxing demands. We live in a country of abundance. There are, indeed, too many choices to make. There are so many options. There is so much good to choose from. There are so many exciting ways to spend our time.

If we want to grow in being best friends in a marriage, we will have to make difficult choices. There will always be an increasing demand on our time for good things, yet things which will eat up all of our time and not allow enough time to build a friendship with our spouses. To build a solid friendship in marriage we must determine first that this relationship is a priority and that we are willing to put time into it.

The challenge to a growing young family is compounded because, as we have seen, our lives in this season are complicated by the many different stresses common to young couples. The tendency can be subtly to put the marriage relationship on hold while we meet the "louder" demands around us. We may find ourselves inadvertently adopting the attitude of "We'll spend time together when things calm down." Things will not calm down in the first dozen years. Life only gets more complicated. When the children do all enter school, the wife may have some greater flexibility, but if the marriage has been neglected during the early years, it will be even easier to continue in the pattern of neglect.

If we want to become best friends in marriage, we must commit to making time together a priority. This will mean saying no to many things we would like to do. It will not be easy. It will sometimes be painful. It may mean giving up a club membership to have time and financial resources to do things together. It may mean saying no to an office expansion. It may mean saying no to an evening with good friends to enable you to go out alone. It may mean saying no to an attractive community project in order not to be overcommitted. Commitment is costly, and we must be willing to pay the price.

There are things that we would like to do that we simply need to postpone until several years down the road when our children are older and gone. Learning to postpone pleasures and satisfaction is an evidence of maturity. Because of the abundance of choices facing couples, we will have to decide to postpone many things that we would enjoy in order to invest that time in each other.

Sometimes we are deceived by the sheer attractiveness of opportunities. The world tells us that we should work harder, produce more, move faster. Instead, what we really need is to simplify and to enjoy. I've never heard of anyone who at the end of their life was heard to say, "I wish I had spent more time on my career, on my house, or on my golf game." Usually, we regret that we did not spend more time with our families.

Mothers who work at home spend time in a child-oriented

environment. While this is good in many ways, it is not good if our children's needs are *always* coming before our spouses'. Our children are on loan to us by God for a very short time before they leave to form their own homes. We will live with our mates for a lifetime though. It is easy to fall into the trap of continually putting our children before our marriage. This is bad for them, and it's bad for us. They need to know that mom and dad are first in each other's lives. This gives them security in a world of broken relationships.

Our calendars will reflect our priorities. If we say that our spouses are important, then time alone with them will show up on our calendars. Before we were married, a wise friend counseled us to take one night a week as a date night to go out alone as a couple to be together, to cultivate the friendship. This was one of the most valuable pieces of advice we got.

Johnny was in school and I was working full-time. We were also involved in a ministry to young people. We kept our commitment though, and that habit made a huge difference when the children started coming, and life got more complicated. When the children arrived, the demands became greater. Ultimately, I needed two babysitters instead of one to manage, and we were tempted many times to say let's forget our date. Sometimes we would, and we would inevitably regret not having had that time together.

In this busy season in our lives, we need to know that we are going to have one block of time each week just to relax and be together to have fun! It should be written on our calendars in advance. This time away enables us to catch our breath, to become reacquainted, and to discuss little issues before they blossom into big problems. It's too easy for us to say we'll schedule time together when things aren't so busy. That time needs to be scheduled now. Our lives will always be busy.

When moms are kept up a lot with nonsleeping babies, there's also the need just to get away and sleep. During our early years, we would find another couple to trade kids with so we could take turns going away for a weekend every three or four months. This is not a luxury; it's a necessity when you have small children. Wives need sleep to be good companions, and husbands and wives need time away together.

There are many ways to spend time together as mates. Each couple must determine what is best for them during the seasons they are in and put it on their calendars now. As the children grow and schedules change, flexibility will be needed in arranging time together. Now that my children are all in school, Johnny and I often have a breakfast date during the week rather than an evening out.

Circumstances will differ for each couple, but the priority of spending time together must remain if you want to build a growing friendship. Pick a time and talk with your spouse about the year ahead, and write down times on your calendar that you can be together as mates. It takes time to become a best friend, and having your mate as your best friend is the richest blessing of all.

Dear Steve:

> After God created man in His own image, He gave him everything He thought he could possibly want and yet man was alone. God saw that this was not good (Genesis 2:18). And so He created a helpmate, or a companion for him. This woman was to be his companion for life and together they would live in God's creation. In a world of broken relationships, God still calls people together in companionship. With the security of permanence in the companionship, we do not fear; with Christ at the center of the friendship, we forgive; with the gift of a companion mate, we experience the rich joys of friendship. In this miracle of relationships we catch a glimpse into the love that surrounds God's relationship with His Son.

Focus Questions

Meditate on Ephesians 4:1-16.

1. How has God called me to walk in my marriage?
2. What gifts do I see that God has given my husband?
3. What gifts do I have that contribute to the marriage?
4. Today I will begin to thank God for one special quality He has given my husband. Each day continue with a different thanksgiving.

Meditate on 1 Corinthians 13:1-8, offering it as a prayer for your marriage.

SOLVING THE DISCIPLINE DILEMMA

Loud screams came bursting from behind the door of the boys' bedroom. Persistent wails and sobs seemed to bounce off every wall of the old Victorian house. These were not the cries of an injured or frightened child. Rather, they were the wails of a very angry two-year-old.

I collapsed in an exhausted heap on the front hall steps. My whole body ached with a sense of defeat. *I'm not sure who is winning this battle of wills—me or my son John*, I thought with a sigh.

First, it had been the cutlery drawers. He was old enough to have learned that these drawers were off-limits to his small hands. He knew he was not allowed to play there. It was dangerous. Instead, he had drawers of pots and plastics where he usually played. This morning, however, he had insisted on playing with the cutlery. Even after a firm warning, he headed straight for the drawer. One spanking and explanation were not enough. He recovered and made a bee-line for the drawer again as if to say, *"We'll see who's boss here."*

Another spanking only seemed to make him more determined. In a fit of anger he ran to the study where he proceeded to pull books off the shelf and throw them on the floor. From previous experience, he knew this too was not allowed.

"John, pick up the books and put them back," I managed to say through clenched teeth as I struggled for control.

"No, Mommy," came the loud authoritative reply. Impudence likewise is not permitted, so off we went to his bedroom with orders to remain until he could learn to obey.

"John," I said, "Mommy loves you very much, but I have to

help you learn to obey." As I sat hunched up on the steps listening
to John's sobs, I had my doubts that I was capable of teaching this
strong-willed child to learn to obey. It had not helped when four-
year-old Allison exclaimed, "Mommy, if you spank John anymore, *I'm* going to cry."

Old familiar doubts began to plague my mind and shake my
self-confidence. Was I too strict? Would I stifle his creativity? Am
I expecting too much or not enough? Why won't he learn the first
time? Have I done something wrong to cause this child to be so
stubborn? How could I know what was the right way to handle
discipline?

Sitting on those steps in a fog of depression, I wondered how
many other mothers of toddlers were being tyrannized by their
children. A loss of confidence is a common plight that many of us
share as we train young children. We want to do what is right as
we discipline the children. However, we frequently don't feel we
know what it is. Or as soon as we have a plan figured out, our
child does something totally unexpected. Or our husbands disagree with us over how to handle a situation. Depression sets in as
our confidence disintegrates.

Crisis of Confidence: Lack of a Strategy

Our toddler may stomp her foot, throw her food, or pinch her
brother. She may make another huge mess in the family room and
refuse to clean it up. How do we respond?

Our small children fuss over a toy, and the disagreement
evolves into a loud fight complete with cruel accusations. An exhausted mother angrily responds with heavy discipline only to ask
herself later, "Did I overreact?"

Alas, in the area of discipline, it is not uncommon to find
ourselves in the role of responders rather than trainers. Frequently, we find ourselves responding to each crisis as it comes
along, perhaps only realizing afterward that we handled it
wrongly. Frustration mounts as we lack a clear sense of direction
in how to implement discipline in the home. Perhaps it seems that
our small children are indeed in control of the household. The
questions seem more numerous than the answers. Who is in control, me or my children? How do I communicate love and teach

obedience at the same time? What expectations should I have of my children?

Our confidence slips another notch as we experience the normal frustrations inherent in raising disciplined children. Our lack of confidence grows because we do not have a strategy for discipline in our homes. In order to be a trainer instead of merely a responder, we need a strategy.

A road map charts the way for a weary traveler. The destination is circled and various routes provide options by which he might proceed. Aimlessness surrounds a traveler who has no destination and no planned course of travel. He feels frustrated and confused as he finds himself merely responding to the different options as they present themselves.

A map, however, instills confidence and allows the freedom from which he is able to choose his particular route. In a similar way, a strategy for discipline and training will offer confidence to the frustrated parent.

Crisis of Confidence: Disunity Between Parents

A couple we'll call Tom and Jane had a strong marriage. Church was a central part of their lives. They eagerly looked forward to having children. When the children arrived, however, they were in for a shock. Jane's philosophy was that of leniency. She believed love meant only understanding and compassion. To her, discipline was unloving. When her toddler did not want to eat his dinner, her response was, "That's all right, honey, you just go play." When the six-year-old did not feel like doing her chores, Jane was very understanding and said, "It's all right, sweetie, you don't have to."

To compensate for Jane's leniency, Tom found himself over-disciplining. He fussed continually at the children. He made unreasonable demands. In an effort to teach them some self-discipline, he overreacted to disobedience with punishment that was too severe.

Caught between two conflicting philosophies, the children soon learned to play the parents against each other. They developed insecurities and began to have trouble in school. Tom and Jane started to blame each other. Their marriage had been so good until they had children. Now the question of discipline became a "sore subject" in their relationship. Their disunity served to increase the tension between them because when one made a decision about discipline, they knew they lacked the support of their mate.

A road map can be of help only as the travelers agree on a common destination. There will be several different routes to take to reach the destination. In order for the trip to be pleasant, however, travelers must discuss and agree upon the best possible route. After listening to each other's suggestions and working together, the travelers can determine the best plan.

In the same way, two parents with differing philosophies on discipline must recognize their different expectations, then decide upon a unified strategy for training their children. This allows a mutual confidence to be restored.

Crisis of Confidence: Confused Goals

It was a beautiful sunny day, the first one to offer a promise of spring and an end to the long cold winter. Several mothers, eager to escape the confinement of the house, headed for the park with their young children. As the moms pushed swings and watched children on jungle gyms, they began to discuss their common efforts to teach their children to obey.

One mother felt that she should allow her child to do anything he pleased that was not physically harmful. She wanted to develop his total creative energies and feared that restrictions might hamper this development. Even the mere words "obey" and "discipline" had negative connotations for her.

Another mom was determined that her daughter become a disciplined singer as she was, and her regime of practice for her daughter left little time for play.

As several other mothers joined in the discussions, it became clear that there was little consensus on the goals of discipline.

Amidst the continual demands of small children, we can become frustrated as we seek to meet their needs. Perhaps we may wonder, *Why am I doing this? How do I know what is right?* It is easy to lose perspective when we are surrounded by toddlers. Our confidence is shaken when another mother at the park challenges us on our views, and we are unable to explain to her why we believe what we do. A lack of clear goals in discipline can cause a drop in confidence.

Just as the map reader must have a destination in mind, so the mother must have clear goals in view if she is to train her children with confidence. Our goals for discipline will be defined as we study God's perspective on discipline.

In order to give confidence to parents in the training of their children, we need a strategy, a plan that will enable parents to be unified and a strategy that will have clear goals. When we study God's Word, we find our goals for discipline. In developing the components of a plan, we will find unity. As we implement the strategy, we will have a clear focus of what to do and why. Finally, once we leave the toddler years, we will be able to see the benefits of a strategy for discipline.

Biblical Basis for Our Strategy

A study of any portion of the Old Testament will give us a glimpse of God's views of discipline. The motivation of God's discipline was and is always *love*. As Proverbs 3:11-12 states, "My son, do not reject the discipline of the Lord / or loathe His reproof. / For whom the Lord loves He reproves. / Even as a father, the son in whom he delights." God's discipline always grows out of love and is for the benefit of His children. Much of God's discipline involves explanation and training.

In observing the relationship God has had with His children from Adam and Eve to the children of Israel, we notice He provides clear instructions. He has clear expectations for behavior and defined consequences for disobedience. Adam and Eve were given everything to enjoy in their beautiful garden. They were allowed to eat from any tree except one. God instructed them not to eat from the tree of the knowledge of good and evil. As we know, they disobeyed and, as a result, suffered the consequences of their actions.

In His dealings with Moses and the children of Israel, God desired what was the absolute best for them. In so doing He gave laws for them to obey. When they obeyed God, they were blessed; when they disobeyed, they suffered. Throughout it all, God's love for them never changed. His discipline was always for their own good.

The writer to the Hebrews explains:

> He disciplines us for our good, that we may share His holiness. All discipline for the moment seems not to be joyful, but sorrowful; yet to those who have been trained by it, afterwards it yields the peaceful fruit of righteousness (Hebrews 12:10-11).

In this passage we find that there are three aspects to godly discipline. First, it is for our own good. Second, it enables us to share God's holiness. And third, it yields the fruit of righteousness.

Through Biblical examples and direct teaching, we see the crucial role of discipline in character development. From Scripture we glimpse the goals of discipline, and we are reminded that the motivation for discipline is love.

Practically, what do these principles really mean? How should they actually affect the way we train our children? First, just as God's discipline springs from love, so too must ours. How well I remember as a child having to be punished and hearing my parents say, "Susan, we are doing this because we love you. We don't like it any more than you do, but we love you and that means we have to help you learn to obey." As a young child I did not understand, but as years passed, understanding began to grow.

Second, in His relationship with His children, God always took much time to explain and to prepare His children to walk in His ways. Much of what Godly discipline involves is *training* and *teaching*. Adequate explanation and anticipation of situations can serve to prevent future situations in which punishment is necessary. It is helpful to see discipline as both training *and* punishment.

Third, our goal in discipline should be twofold: to train in *self-discipline* and to teach obedience. When our children learn self-discipline at an early age, they will be more likely to withstand the temptations of sin as they grow up. They will also have the personal discipline to be productive adults. Obedience to God is first learned when a child is taught obedience to his parents. If a child does not learn to obey his parents whom he sees, how can he be expected to obey a God whom he cannot see?

As our children learn self-discipline and obedience, they will be enabled to share in God's holiness and to see for themselves the benefits of leading a disciplined life. The result of this training will be children who have learned the joy and the freedom of obedience, children who become the adults that God has created them to be, and who have the privilege of being His messengers of hope to a world in need.

With this "destination" in mind, we are able to determine the components of a strategy for teaching discipline to our small children.

Components of a Discipline Strategy

As parents develop a plan for discipline, they need to do three things: define clear expectations, determine procedures, and draw helpful distinctions.

Define Clear Expectations

It is difficult to define clear expectations for children whose parents do not share the same philosophy. Tom and Jane had been raised in families whose views on discipline were at opposite poles. They came into marriage with different viewpoints on the best way to raise their children. Conflict arose because they did not discuss these differences or seek help.

When conflict arises between mates, it is crucial to discuss the differences. Looking back at how we were raised may be especially enlightening. What did our parents expect from us? How was my training helpful or harmful in preparing me for adulthood? In what ways do we want our home to be *different* from the homes in which we were raised?

If we desire to have a Christian home, we must look first to God's Word in designing a plan for discipline. Husbands and wives together should study Bible passages that relate to discipline. Choose several books that discuss building strong Christian families and read them together. In addition, seek out an older couple who have raised their children effectively and ask their advice.

In solving this potential "sore subject," we should apply the same principle that we would in our careers when faced with opposing viewpoints. Articulate the problem, do research, and come up with a unified plan. Parents must overcome their disagreements if they are to provide a positive discipline experience in the home. As parents work together toward a unified plan, it is helpful to agree on the basic expectations we have in training our children. Three common expectations might be honesty, courtesy, and responsibility. In discussing these expectations, it is helpful to note a difference between expected behavior and normal behavior.

It is normal for our small child to lie, but we must expect him to become honest. From the first lie, the small child should be taught that this behavior is not permissible. Honesty is the expectation in this household.

Courtesy will probably be another expectation in our homes. Rudeness and impudence will be normal reactions for a toddler. However, he should be trained from the beginning that this behavior is not acceptable. Instead, politeness is expected.

Responsibility is a trait we seem to be forever teaching our children. They will naturally be irresponsible by making a mess and leaving it for mom to clean up, or by throwing a tantrum in the shopping center. Part of training is teaching them personal responsibility.

Honesty, courtesy, and responsibility are just three examples of expectations. There will be others. Talking through our expectations with our mate will be a must. When we agree on the expectations we have of our children, we will then be able to determine together the procedures necessary in training our children to meet these expectations.

1. Determine Procedures

We never knew when we became mothers that we would have so many different job descriptions—chauffeur, manager, counselor, financial advisor, caterer, and maid are but a few of the roles we are called to fulfill. A primary role we often do not consider is that of *teacher*. Even though some are professionally trained as teachers, all mothers are cast in the role of teacher. We need to see this role as an exciting opportunity to mold a child. Indeed, this is the positive aspect of discipline.

First, the teaching aspect of discipline involves clear explanations and positive reinforcement. Once we know what we expect of our children, we must be certain that we communicate these expectations clearly to them. We also need to be sure that they understand. It is easy for a misunderstanding to develop into a confrontation when the whole thing could have been avoided had the parties communicated clearly. Children appreciate knowing what is expected of them. Confusion breeds insecurity. Clearly articulating our wishes is a first step in training our children.

2. Reinforce the Positives

Positive reinforcement is another tool which enables the teaching of our children to be a pleasant experience. Verbal praise for a job well done lights up the countenance of a three-year-old and encourages him to do it again. Written notes of praise or a star chart with stickers for chores well done are positive ways of reinforcing good behavior. Hugs, kisses, and a phone call to Grandma to brag about a child's accomplishment as he listens are all ways to say "I'm proud of you" and build self-esteem.

When we provide clear explanations and positive reinforcement as valuable teaching tools, it will make the more unpleasant aspects of discipline seem less awful.

3. Establish Consequences

Establishing consequences is a procedure that should be agreed upon by the parents and which must be clearly explained to the children. Limits on behavior must be established and the consequences of misbehavior carefully explained to all. Then the parents must follow through with the consequences.

Unfortunately, this is where a breakdown in the system often occurs. Changing procedures midstream or failing to follow through with punishments causes general confusion on the part of the child. He will not know what response his behavior will bring. In addition, failure to follow through will ultimately cause the parents to lose credibility with their child.

Max is a strong, feisty beagle puppy who recently arrived as a surprise at my friend Jackie's house. With four children to train, Jackie already had her hands full. Max, however, moved in with "control" in his beady eyes. He climbed on the furniture, chewed up the shoes, teethed on the children, messed where he pleased, and did not come when called. After consulting a dog trainer, the family decided to adopt a new strategy. They began to let Max know that he was not the boss of the house. When he misbehaved, he received a quick punishment. At once, his behavior began to change radically for the better. Now when he misbehaved he expected a punishment and received it.

As the family established consequences and followed through with punishment, Max became a happier dog and family life greatly improved.

Spanking and withdrawing privileges are the two consequences to misbehavior that are the most effective. The age of the child and the extent of the misbehavior should determine the consequence. Some parents have found a spanking spoon or a switch to be more effective than the hand. I always used the hand because I never could find the others when they were needed. The tool does not make that much difference. The punishment does. Unfortunately, some have taught that spanking is unloving and unwise. In fact, it is just the opposite. A two-year-old will not fully understand adult reasoning. He's not supposed to! He will, however, get the message that the spanking will bring. His bad behavior brought unpleasant consequences. Spanking is helpful because it clearly communicates, it is swift, then it is over. When it is over, a big hug offers reassurance. Spanking can be a positive force in teaching self-discipline and obedience.

Recently, four-year-old Elizabeth Ann had a very bad day. She was exceptionally naughty and received several spankings in a brief period. In addition, she was not allowed to attend a birthday party that afternoon. It was a difficult, unpleasant time for both mother and child. However, it soon ended and as the two of them had a tea party together, Elizabeth Ann said to her mom, "Mom, I was just using up all my badness on you!"

Our children know when they are disobedient, and a swift spanking may be painful for the moment, but it is also temporary. A swift consequence enables the issue to be forgotten and prevents resentment from being built up.

Withdrawal of privileges becomes effective as the child's reasoning powers mature and his interests and activities increase (usually around age four or five). We found the first four years to be the most crucial in establishing and carrying out consequences for misbehavior. These are the years it seems we are forever punishing our children. Yet if we are firm in these years, there will be a marked decrease in the need for punishment as the child turns five and six. Much of the battle is won, and the child has begun to learn the value of self-discipline and obedience.

4. Use Preventative Measures

Utilizing preventative measures is a final aspect in determining discipline procedures. Routine, diversion, and anticipation are three preventative measures which are especially helpful.

Small children adjust to a regular routine. Hassled moms work best within the framework of a routine. Knowing that meals are at a specified time and that bedtime is regular will help prevent unnecessary confrontations. Naptime which is regular will become expected and offer rest to weary children and mothers. A structure offers security because the child knows what is expected. Reading stories at bedtime or singing at meals are routines that become special and bring joy to all.

Diversion offers another preventative measure in discipline training. When your nine-month-old heads for the green potted plants, it is best to remove the plants and get out the blocks. When she wants to play with knives and forks, fill a drawer with plastic containers instead. Any time we can substitute one safe activity for a dangerous endeavor, we are practicing diversion. Diversion is a tremendous positive aid, but it cannot ultimately replace firm training. Once the child's ability to understand "yes" and "no" is clear, limits must be set, and a trip to the cutlery drawer should bring a firmer punishment. Diversion is, however, a help especially in the early months.

Anticipation is a tool that can be used for every age. Anticipation involves creatively planning ahead to avoid unpleasant circumstances. Anticipation can be used in everyday situations and for special occasions. For example, your three-year-old child has given up the need for afternoon naps. However, the baby still naps and you would love some peace and quiet yourself. Explain to your child that even though he does not have to sleep, he gets to have a "rest time." In anticipating a fuss that might occur at "rest time," create some positive activities for the three-year-old to do on his bed. Favorite books and a "rest-time" craft box will make this a more pleasant experience. An alarm clock that he can watch will notify him when his "rest time" is over.

During vacation, an "illness" seems to strike most families. At our house it's known as the "there's-nothing-to-do syndrome." As summer vacation approaches, there is great excitement and expectancy. But then when that long-awaited first day of summer finally arrives, the dread "disease" strikes. "There's nothing to do, Mom." Expectations are dashed, and the joy of freedom can decline into the "disease" of boredom.

In anticipation of this "disease," we take some time before summer vacation (or holidays in the winter) to meet as a family and list all of the activities available during the vacation. We take a larger poster board and write down Things to Do by Myself, Things to Do with Friends, and Things to Do in Bad Weather. Planning becomes a game in which we see how creative we can be. We then post the list for reference. When the "disease" strikes, the children are reminded to check the list. Anticipating the problem and creating solutions in advance will serve as a preventative measure.

In some cases, merely anticipating unusual situations and recognizing them as normal will help us deal with unpleasant circumstances. Often, after a holiday, short trip, or any change in routine, children will tend to misbehave for several days. I call this the "re-entry syndrome." When families are away on vacation, a new routine is present. Mom usually has Dad to help and the children have more attention. Upon returning home, Dad goes back to the office, and Mom resumes her responsibilities. It simply takes about three days of re-entry to adjust. It is best to relax and to plan a quieter routine to enable re-entry to pass quickly.

Simple anticipation of different situations allows us to understand and enables us to plan creatively some ways to avoid unpleasant confrontations. Routine, diversion, and anticipation are three preventative measures in our strategy for discipline.

5. Draw Helpful Distinctions

In determining our plan for discipline, recognizing basic distinctions can be important. Distinguishing between willful disobedience and mistakes will enable a mother to know how to handle the situation. Willful disobedience occurs when the child knows that he is disobeying. When you tell your child to stay in the yard and he goes next door, it's willful disobedience. When your toddler spills his milk at the table, it's a mistake. The consequences for willful disobedience should be firm and swift, whereas those for mistakes lenient and educational. (Move the milk next time!)

Closely related is the distinction between critical issues and secondary issues. A critical issue is one of paramount importance—for example, lying. On the other hand, a secondary issue is not so vital. The five-year-old's desire to wear clothes that don't match would be a secondary issue. Parents need to emphasize the critical issues as we train our children. We want to avoid having too many rules. It is impossible to enforce too many, and it makes the atmosphere in our homes become negative. It is far better to consistently enforce the critical issues and be willing to let some of the secondary ones slide.

A final distinction we need to make is between real needs and felt needs. A toddler may feel he must have a cookie when his real need is for dinner. Parents are better equipped to determine the child's real needs than the child is. Asking ourselves the question, "Is this a real need or a felt need?" will often enable us to more clearly evaluate a child's demand.

All of these distinctions will be extremely helpful when our children become teenagers. As we begin to utilize these distinctions in our own thinking when our children are small, we will benefit as they get older. Determining the components of a discipline strategy is the first step toward a beneficial plan. Implementing the strategy is another story altogether. That involves confidence, conviction, and creativity.

Implementing a Discipline Strategy

Communicating clear expectations, following through with consequences, maintaining balance, and allowing for failure are four aspects to implementing our discipline strategy.

Communicate Clear Expectations

Just as it is important for the parents to agree on expectations like honesty, courtesy, and responsibility, it is vital that we communicate these expectations to our children.

Dinner was over and I carefully put the extra piece of cake on the counter to save for the next day. Several hours later I returned to find crumbs scattered about the counter. My young son approached with a mouth encircled with chocolate and a satisfied grin on his face.

"Son, did you eat the cake?" I asked.

"No, Mama," came the reply.

"Son, it is important to tell the truth. If you ate the cake, you must tell Mommy. If you ate the cake and you tell me that you did not, that is a lie. It is wrong. I'm going to ask you again. Did you eat the cake?"

"Yes, Mommy," came a sob.

"Now, I'm glad you told me the truth. Because this is the first time, I will not punish you, but next time you do not tell the truth, I will punish you. We must always tell the truth. Do you understand?"

The next time our child lies, we must follow through with an appropriate punishment. Our explanation and expectations are clear. Honesty is a value we uphold.

Courtesy is another common value. Our children will be likely to pick up bad language from different places. When they come home with some expression that is wrong, we need to tell them that those words are unacceptable. We do not want to hear them anymore. A traditional—and, I might add, very effective—solution for bad language is washing a mouth out with soap. Let the child know that this is what will happen the next time we hear bad words. It will probably not happen more than once!

Making sure that our children understand what is expected of them is the first step in the implementation of a discipline strategy. But, second, it is vital that we follow through with consequences for their behavior.

Follow Through with Consequences

Many questions concerning the implementation of discipline center around how best to follow through and what punishment is appropriate for what age. When we attempt to follow through with punishment, a question frequently heard is, "How many times should I warn my child or tell him to do something before I expect him to obey?"

Our child learns when he must obey by our response. One little boy was heard to say, "I don't have to obey until Mommy puts on her mad voice." If we want to avoid becoming nagging mothers, we should explain to our children that we will ask them to do something no more than twice, then they will have to suffer the consequences if they do not obey.

"Son, turn the television off, please." If it is not turned off immediately, tell him once more. "Son, I said turn the television off, please." If he does not obey then, he should be punished.

In teaching our children to obey, we must keep in mind that we are building for the future. It may be tedious and unpleasant at the moment, but our goal is an obedient, self-disciplined adult.

In considering the appropriate punishment for each age, the guideline to use is the child's level of comprehension. When it becomes apparent that the toddler understands "no," it is appropriate to begin to discipline him when he does something to which you have given him a warning. As their understanding grows, we expect better obedience. Balance is essential because we do not want to have too many "no's." In the beginning with small children, "no" will usually refer to dangerous items like the hot stove or the electric outlet. As they grow, the issues will become more complex. But the principle of clear explanation, one warning, and follow-through should remain.

When a child develops special interests and is involved in different activities, the withholding of privileges becomes an effective consequence of misbehavior. A friend with three children allows each of her children to invite a special friend over one day each week to play. This is a privilege which they look forward to. Lately her children have begun to fight with one another. She explained that if they fought, they would forego the privilege of having a friend over that week. Once they did fight and consequently lost this privilege. Since then, the household fights have showed a marked decrease.

There will be times when we ask our child to do something and the response is, "I don't feel like it," or "I don't want to." We must explain that there are many things in life that we don't feel like doing or that we don't want to do. Mommies don't often feel like cooking, but we do it anyway. We must instill in our children that they do things because they are right, not necessarily because they always feel like it. This is an important element in training in self-discipline.

There will inevitably be those cases when our best attempts to explain our expectations and follow through with appropriate punishment seem to fail. The bedtime battle is one of those times in which mothers of small children often feel defeated. We put them to bed. Then they need water. They need to potty. Or they want more cover. It can go on and on until it becomes a contest that the child enjoys and the mother dreads.

One friend with two small boys said that she found that if she took care of the necessities first, it was preventative discipline. She then told each boy they could take one toy or book into bed to play with for fifteen minutes. They were not to get out of bed. After fifteen minutes the light went out. If they got up again or turned the light back on, they were spanked. We cannot make our children sleep, but we can teach them to obey in going to bed. We must determine to persist in this training no matter how long it takes.

When our children were toddlers, I often found that I was being victimized by what I call the "terminal whines." After trying several solutions to this problem, we decided that if anyone had a case of the whines, he had to go to his room until the illness went away. Mom included. More than once my oldest daughter has said, "Mom, you need to go to your room." She was right.

Shopping malls and grocery stores become favorite places for children to misbehave. When this happens, simply take the child to the car or to the restroom and discipline him. Inasmuch as we are able, we should discipline our children in private. However, they must learn that being in a public place will not protect them from deserved discipline.

When we are faced with a situation that seems to defy a solution, it is helpful to ask ourselves if we have explained clearly to our child the behavior we expect and the consequences for misbehavior. Have we followed through with discipline as necessary?

Take heart, challenging situations will stump every mother. At some time, each of us will feel that our creative child is out to sabotage every strategy we have. Now is the time to sit back and laugh—so we won't cry—and call up a friend saying, "Would you believe this?" We will survive and our child will, too. By the time we leave this season, that challenging situation will become a humorous memory.

Two final aspects in implementing a discipline strategy involve maintaining balance and allowing for failure.

Maintain Balance

As parents we want to avoid the extremes of being too strict or too lenient.

A parent that is too strict is one who is frequently saying "no," giving orders, and attempting to enforce too many rules. The atmosphere in that home will be negative. A child will develop the feeling that nothing he can do will be good enough to please his parents. Punishment may be too severe for the offense committed. The parent will find herself feeling like a general dispensing orders right and left. Her children may become withdrawn and fearful or rebellious.

On the other hand, a parent who is too lenient will produce obnoxious children. Her home will be ruled by a child who knows he is the boss. Rudeness and backtalk will be common. Temper tantrums will become manipulative tools to force parents to give in. The result will be selfish, demanding children who become adults that expect other people to cater to them.

What we desire is balance. Our homes should be places where "yes" is most frequently heard, where expected behavior is understood and enforced. The parents should be in control and thus respected by their children. The home will then be characterized by love, joy, and controlled chaos. Maintaining balance involves recognizing the extremes and seeking to implement a consistent strategy of love and discipline.

Consistency in itself is a great challenge for weary mothers. From time to time we all find ourselves being inconsistent in our training. Typical causes of inconsistency are fatigue, inexperience, and lack of a strategy. One day we might send our child to his room for hitting his brother. The next day, exhausted from being a referee, we simply ignore the fighting. If this inconsistent response on our part continues, our children will be confused as to what behavior is acceptable. However, we must realize that tired moms make mistakes, but if these mistakes are the exception rather than the norm, they do not produce damaging results. Simply recognize the tendency, get some rest, and determine to be more consistent.

In our experience as moms, we may find ourselves being quite strict with our first child and too lenient with our last. This can be good or bad. New mothers do tend to try too hard, and we need to relax and not take our jobs too seriously. On the other hand, we should not so wear out by the time the last child arrives that we unconsciously permit behavior that has been wrong for our other children.

Being aware of these tendencies and making an effort to adjust our expectations will help restore balance. Finally, inconsistent parenting results because we do not have a working strategy. When we find ourselves being inconsistent, we need to reexamine our strategy and seek to implement a plan that encourages consistency.

Allow for Failure

There's tremendous pressure today to "succeed" in some way, shape, or form. Our children are more driven and more serious than we were at their age. When we moms were pregnant, we all prayed fervently for just a healthy baby. After the healthy baby arrived, that wasn't enough. The child needed to be bright, beautiful, have friends, excel in school, and do well in the world. There is not much room for "failure." Then sometimes when the child fails, the parents are either furious with the child or rush out to blame the teacher or the neighborhood child or someone else for their child's problems.

Allowing our children to fail is a necessary part of their growth. It is wrong for parents to cover up for or to bail out their kids. We once had a neighbor whose teenage son got in a great deal of trouble with the law. In his early years of misbehavior, his father set limits for his behavior, but the father never followed through. Consequently, the son did not learn to be responsible for his actions. His dad always got him out of trouble. The son said to us, "My dad will fix things for me."

I meet weekly with a group of women for prayer. We all have children in the same public schools, and we come together to pray for our schools, teachers, staff, and our children. Recently as we were together, one of the moms prayed, "Lord, if any of our children are doing something they should not be, help them to get caught!" One child did get caught sharing homework notes with a friend. As she and her parents worked through this situation, many positive lessons were learned. The family became closer and the child grew in accepting responsibility for her behavior. It is indeed a blessing when our young children get caught in their misbehavior. When they are small, their behavior is more easily changed because we have a greater influence in shaping them.

When our children make wrong decisions and experience failure, we need to comfort them in their pain and be with them as they take their punishment or make their restitution, loving them in the midst of it. Yet we must also help them to learn accountability for their actions and to think about future ramifications of their failure. For example, how would they do things differently next time? Failing at something can produce a great time for discussion and creative problem solving. It will also help teach us sympathy and empathy for others' failures.

In attempting to implement our discipline strategy, we too will fail. This is natural. After all, we have no prior experience in parenting, and we have not exactly taken many courses on discipline training. Our strategy is meant to be a vehicle that produces confidence. It is not a set of laws that we must keep. Rather, it is like the road map that plots the best route to our destination. In so doing, the travelers enjoy the trip because they know where they are going and how.

We will make mistakes, we will experience frustration, and we too will fail. However, God is bigger than all of our failures and He can fix anything. As we attempt to implement a plan, we should not be discouraged, but be encouraged knowing that we will experience many benefits from a discipline strategy.

Benefits of a Discipline Strategy

The most obvious benefit of a strategy for discipline is the confidence that the plan enables the parents to have. No longer are we merely responders to the challenges of discipline, rather we are trainers. We have a sense of control, and we know where we are headed and why. We understand God's perspective on discipline, and as we work with our husbands, we are able to become unified in our own plans. Unity brings a sense of camaraderie. Knowing we have a soulmate who will support us greatly encourages us during the difficult times. In turn, we can be encouragers to our single-parent friends.

Not only is confidence a benefit, but also personal growth in discipline will be a benefit. It is not effective to attempt to train our children in self-discipline and obedience without growing in these areas ourselves.

For example, as we struggle to bring some difficult task to completion, we are exhibiting self-discipline. It's special to share our own frustrations with a child and have them pray for us as we continue with our project. When we stick to our priorities in an act of obedience, perhaps giving up an interesting opportunity for a more important one, we are growing in obedience ourselves. Growing in self-discipline and obedience is a life-long process for parents and children. As the children grow up we become companions in this process with similar goals in mind. What a blessing this is.

Confidence and personal growth are two benefits a strategy will produce for parents. We will also be encouraged as we see several results in the lives of our children.

A strategy provides the opportunity for a child to grow in his self-worth. His personal security increases as he understands the limits that control his behavior. Knowing what is expected of him will dissolve confusion and enable freedom. As he grows in responsibility, his self-confidence will increase. In learning self-discipline, he will discover his own productive capabilities.

We will notice a second benefit of our strategy as we watch our children enter adolescence. The training in self-discipline and obedience will equip them for living in a world full of temptations. With a foundation of self-discipline, they will be better able to discern and to say "no" to things that are not right.

As we begin to watch them make difficult choices we will be thankful for those early years when we persisted in training, even though we often wanted to quit. Their choices will not always be right, but a background of self-discipline and obedience will enable them to have clear convictions and a strong will.

Finally, the most precious result of our training will be watching our children gradually shift from obeying their parents who love them to obeying their Heavenly Father who loves them even more.

Solving the discipline dilemma begins with a strategy based on the principles of God's Word. The strategy enables the parents to have a plan that will function as a guideline to a richer, more enjoyable season with our young children.

Focus Questions

Meditate on Colossians 3:1-17.

1. As we train our children, what character traits do we want to help them turn away from?
2. Which qualities do we desire for them to cultivate?
3. In what areas do we need to be more consistent in our training this week?
4. What specific strategy will I adopt to help me be more consistent?

Meditate on 2 Peter 1:1-11, making this a prayer for each child.

SEVEN

CREATING A LOVING ATMOSPHERE IN THE HOME

Our car turned up the narrow driveway leading to a large old brick house. Johnny and I were eagerly anticipating our visit with Tucker and Ginny and their children. Two dogs greeted us with loud barks, and a cat darted across the path as we honked the horn to announce our arrival.

The front door of the house flew open and out rushed two little girls ages seven and five. Close behind were Ginny, carrying the baby, and Tucker, who hoisted a two-year-old on his shoulders. Huge grins and warm hugs made us feel welcomed as everyone began to talk at once.

Johnny and I were still newlyweds, having been married barely a year. We had begun to think about starting our own family, and a visit to Tucker and Ginny's busy household was both encouraging and overwhelming. As I watched Ginny, I would marvel, "How in the world does she do it?" Their home radiated a sense of happy confusion. All eight of us gathered around the large old kitchen table topped with two huge homemade chicken pies. There seemed to be kids everywhere. With hearts full of thanksgiving we joined hands and prayed, thanking God for His many blessings and for the delicious food.

The dinner was punctuated with much humor. A two-year-old's messy face and feeble attempts to get more in his mouth than on the table sent us all into fits of laughter. Throughout the meal the children joined in the conversations. There was a sense that whatever they said was important. Each member of the family was treated with honor. There was a genuine naturalness as the family members related to one another. This is what I want my family to be like, I thought, as I soaked up the loving atmosphere at the dinner table. There was something special here, something unique, and it felt good. I sensed love, acceptance, and joy.

I'd been to other homes where walking through the front door resembled entering a fog of depression. The mother was unhappy and one imagined that she felt resigned to an unpleasant task. The children turned deaf ears to her continual nagging. Their play was punctuated with phrases of "shut up" and "you're stupid." Mealtime was an ordeal to hurry through rather than a time of enjoyment. Rudeness was common and ignored. Sarcasm replaced laughter. The tired, battle-weary parents rarely smiled. Instead, it seemed their season of small children was a test of endurance. The atmosphere in their home made one feel sad.

Recognizing seasons is important, establishing priorities is essential, and acquiring realistic expectations is helpful. Yet the atmosphere in which all this takes place is crucial in determining the emotional well being of the family members. Our homes will never be perfect places. However, the atmosphere that marks the home will determine whether it is a positive happy place, a place that offers shelter from the world, a place where we can have our batteries recharged to go out again.

Our homes should encourage humor, appreciation, forgiveness, a sense of belonging, where we are believed in and accepted. Creating a home with such an atmosphere of love, forgiveness, and laughter brings healing into a broken world.

As mothers we have the major responsibility of creating the atmosphere in the home. Of course our husbands contribute, but we are usually at home more than they are. This is a true privilege, not a burden. Just as we often assume the initiative in planning the decor of our homes, we also have the opportunity to determine what kind of atmosphere we want for our homes.

I have a pot of "smells" that I like to keep simmering on my stove. The ingredients in the pot are cinnamon, cloves, and allspice. When mixed together in a small amount of water and left to cook, these ingredients produce a most pleasing fragrance. The spicy aroma permeates the entire house. More than once my children have come home to say, "Mom, this house stinks. You need to put the smells pot on."

Sometimes I have not noticed when my home has an unpleasant aroma. Perhaps it's musty or just stale. Occasionally, when I'm cooking I get so accustomed to the different smells that I do not recognize that the overall effect is unpleasant.

The atmosphere in our homes can become unpleasant, too, without our even realizing it. Harsh talk and rudeness may become so familiar that we turn a deaf ear to its clamor and do nothing about it. We may not recognize some of the unpleasant qualities in our homes until we visit another home whose atmosphere is pleasant, and we realize that we have neglected to work on our own.

Often we fail to realize that creating a loving atmosphere in the home takes work. It does not just happen. We must have a vision of the atmosphere we desire, goals to work toward, and a plan of action.

In 2 Corinthians 2:14-16, Paul refers to us as a "fragrance" through whom God will manifest the "sweet aroma" of Himself in every place. How wonderful it would be if this "sweet aroma" of God Himself would permeate our homes. What sweet joy and peace would then characterize our homes.

Is it possible to have this aroma of Christ in our homes? What ingredients would be found in an atmosphere where the fragrance of Christ was present? In Galatians 5:22-23 and 1 Corinthians 13:4-8, we have the answer: a list of ingredients for an atmosphere that reflects the presence of Christ.

> The fruit of the Spirit is love, joy, peace, patience, kindness, goodness, faithfulness, gentleness, and self-control.
>
> Love is patient, love is kind, and is not jealous; love does not brag and is not arrogant, does not act unbecomingly; it does not seek its own, is not provoked, and does not take into account a wrong suffered, does not rejoice in unrighteousness but rejoices with the truth; bears all things, believes all things, hopes all things, endures all things. Love never fails.

In these passages we have a beautiful picture of the atmosphere we wish would characterize our homes. As we focus on even just a few of these ingredients, we will gain understanding of how God creates the ingredients, and we will be enabled to develop a practical plan to help produce these qualities in our homes.

Love

Small children take toys away from each other. Elementary school children say very cruel things to their friends. Adolescents form exclusive cliques. Adults often find themselves caught up in negative gossip. The world can be a brutal place where love is lost in the day's events. In this very same world we have the audacity to attempt to create a home whose atmosphere radiates love. Indeed, this will involve a supernatural effort.

If we want to see love characterize our homes, we must first understand and accept God's unconditional love for us. The ultimate expression of God's love is found in John 15:13: "Greater love has no one than this, that one lay down his life for his friends." Romans 5:8 states, "But God demonstrates His own love towards us, in that while we were yet sinners, Christ died for us." Christ speaking in John 15:9 says, "Just as the Father has loved Me, I have also loved you; abide in My love."

It is often hard for us to believe that God would love us totally if He really knew us. In each of our lives there are things that we see that we don't like. There are things that make us feel guilty. There are attitudes that embarrass us. There are thoughts that we would never want anyone else to know about.

But, of course, God does know us totally. He knows those thoughts, those attitudes, and those things we've done and wish we had not done. The amazing thing is that He does know us, and He still loves us. He knows when we get fed up, when we fail, when we lose patience, when we think awful things. Yet He still loves us completely and totally. Nothing we do or don't do can change His love for us. We can't add to it or take away from it.

As we abide first in the security of knowing that God loves us, we will be enabled to allow this love to become an ingredient in our homes. When God's love begins to permeate the atmosphere of our homes, it will produce three characteristics.

Love Is Sacrifice

It was snowing unusually hard for Washington, D.C. School was canceled, businesses were closed. Even our powerful federal government could do nothing to halt the small gentle white flakes of our omnipotent God. A blizzard was in the making.

Our children were ecstatic about the unplanned holiday. We decided it would be fun to take a family hike down Main Street in the middle of the storm. With hats pulled low and boots hiked up, we started out on our winter walk.

Our stroll took us past a street that had a slight incline. Many automobiles were stuck as the motorists tried in vain to get up the hill. Looking at the mess, we noticed two young men in the middle of the street who were helping the stalled motorists get their cars moving up the hill. As I pointed this out to my sons, they said, "They must be making a lot of money." The boys completely missed the point that the men were doing it just to help.

Sadly, the joy of serving seems to be vanishing. Individual rights have taken over. The phrase "inalienable rights" has long meant a sacred trust, protection, and freedom. However, to this sacred trust has been added a new interpretation of individual rights, which is based on self-centeredness. "I have a right to do what's best for me. I have a right to personal happiness." Because it is termed a "right," we may fail to recognize selfishness for what it is.

By including the selfishness of self-seeking in the term individual rights, we neglect to recognize it as sin. When man's self-pleasing becomes a "noble trait," the words sacrifice and servant disappear, and true love is no longer possible.

We see this phenomenon in our own homes. A wife might expect her husband to help with getting the children into bed while he assumes it's his "right" to relax after a long day at work. Our son refuses to do the dinner dishes because it's not "his job." Our daughter won't help babysit the small children because it "interferes" with her plans.

We must return to the principle of sacrifice in our homes if we want the atmosphere in our homes to be characterized by real love instead of fickled sentimentality. The Gospel message is one of sacrifice. The entire Bible is a story of sacrificial love.

Two different examples of sacrifice are illustrated by the lives of Rebekah and Christ.

In one of his last acts before he died, Abraham sent his chief servant back to his own country to find a wife from among their own relatives for his son Isaac. With ten loaded camels, the servant came to the spring at Nahor. As he stopped, he prayed that

God would reveal to him the right wife for Isaac by having a girl not only give him a drink at the well but also offer to water all of his camels. In this way he would know God's choice for Isaac.

Immediately, lovely Rebekah appeared at the well and gave the servant a drink from her jar. She then offered to water his camels, and the excited servant knew that God had answered his prayer. When Rebekah offered to water the ten camels, she was not undertaking an easy job. She was making a big sacrifice. It is not unusual for a thirsty camel to drink three gallons of water at one time. Abraham's servant had ten thirsty camels. Each gallon of water weighed approximately eight pounds. In watering the camels, Rebekah had to lift nearly 240 pounds of water! The water had to be drawn from a deep well and then given to the camels. This was not an easy job. It was a big sacrifice of time and energy.

Rebekah did what she did with no thought of personal gain. She had no idea who the man was or what he wanted. She was simply being a servant.

Jesus' entire life was one of service. Indeed, His death was the ultimate sacrifice. In the story of the footwashing told in John 13, we see one illustration of Jesus as a servant. During his final passover meal with His disciples, Jesus took a towel and began to wash each of their feet. Foot washing was a common occurrence in Jerusalem because everyone wore sandals and the roads were dirty and dusty. This chore was usually reserved for the lowest servant. It was a humbling, unpleasant task.

In washing their feet, Jesus was trying to illustrate to His disciples the importance of being a servant. In sacrificing His dignity to wash their feet, He was preparing them for His ultimate sacrifice on the cross.

We cannot have love without sacrifice. How then can we help sacrifice and service become a reality in our families?

Elisabeth Elliot has said that it takes a secure person to become a servant. Christ knew who He was and where He was going (see John 13:3). Rebekah knew her destiny was in God's hands. As we have confidence that we belong to Christ, we too can grow in becoming servants. Living by the priorities He has given us enables us to have confidence. Being a servant will never be easy. It will not be natural for us or for our children. We are all self-centered and naturally inclined to please ourselves. Making sacrifices hurts. Serving may involve pain. Sacrifice is not convenient nor does it guarantee reward. It caused great discomfort for Rebekah and death for Christ. We must not wait until we feel like serving our mates or our children, because it will never happen. We become servants out of conviction.

It is helpful to view our serving as an offering to God. Mothers with small children are forced to be servants as we care for their needs. We do it because we are committed to and responsible for them. We will get tired of serving, and we will feel unappreciated. If we view service as an offering to God, our focus will shift from ourselves to God, and joy will accompany our duties.

One of the ways we communicate love to our mates is by serving them. My husband loves to have the steps outside our front door swept clean. The inside of the house is more important to me, so I often forget to sweep the walk. He knows this, so when I do try to remember to sweep the walk, he appreciates it. It is the many little things in marriage that either fan the flame of love or extinguish it. Setting aside our rights in order to serve our husbands will fan the flame. It is helpful to ask the question, "What could I do this day to serve my husband?"

Our children desperately need to learn the joy of serving. Today there is much pressure on young people to plan for a good career or to make money. We must begin when they are very young to train them in the importance of service. Family chores are the most obvious places that serving can begin. Even when a toddler is very small, he can still learn to make his bed and pick up his toys. When they begin school, children can learn to fix their own lunches. Every child should have chores that he or she is responsible to do on a regular basis.

In addition, we want our children to learn to be servants in other areas, to do more than what is expected of them. Using the element of surprise can make serving more fun in busy households.

Once the twins helped me clean the boys' room while they were at camp to surprise them. We did tell them that we had a surprise waiting for them—this assured that they would notice and appreciate what was done. The boys were suitably pleased when they returned, and the girls felt appreciated. A surprise plate of homemade cookies prepared for big brothers by little sisters communicates love. Getting up extra early to have time to fix your younger sister's hair is a true sacrifice. Children need to learn to serve each other.

One of the unusual areas in which our children are learning this is in the area of homework. Once they begin sixth grade, the math is beyond me and Johnny! We've established a homework helping order. It's Allison's responsibility to help John; John helps Chris; and Chris—poor Chris—helps both twins! This greatly relieves me, and the children are learning how to serve one another.

Appreciation always makes serving easier, and small children especially need it. However, as the children grow, they must learn that serving will not always be appreciated or recognized. Encouraging your son to shovel the snow from a neighbor's walk is an example of serving without receiving credit. Putting away your brother's or sister's clothes without being asked is serving in the family.

The area of finances offers an opportunity to teach the principle of sacrifice. When the children begin to receive an allowance, they should also begin to tithe—giving back to the Lord ten percent. Beginning this habit as a young child will make it much easier as an adult. It is not negotiable. It is just something we do. In this way a tithe can be a beginning from which to increase our giving rather than a goal to work toward. In addition, it's meaningful to try to contribute additional monies to special needs, like sending other kids to Christian camps or helping a friend in need buy groceries. Doing this anonymously and having the children contribute their few dollars will involve them with us and allow them to share in the joy of giving without recognition.

One family in our neighborhood spends Saturday mornings together working in the yard at the church. Hardly anyone knows that they do this. It's just their act of family service for their church. Encouraging your children to babysit occasionally for free, to rake a neighbor's yard without pay, to donate their allowance to a needy ministry will all help in teaching the principle of sacrifice.

One other element of sacrifice that must be mentioned is the sacrifice of prayer. Prayer is hard work. It takes time. There is no personal material gain. It goes unnoticed by all but God. Yet it is the greatest thing we can do for those we love.

My grandmother died when she was ninety-two. She was a godly woman. As long as I can remember she had a habit of awakening about 4:30 a.m. to pray. She spent much time praying for her family. Countless people have benefited from her prayers. Her sacrificial prayer has been a real example to me.

A house where the atmosphere is marked by the ingredient of love will be a home where its members are learning to be servants.

Love Is Acceptance

Driving home after a disappointing basketball game Chris turned to me and said with great sadness, "Mom, I'm sorry that I played so badly."

"Son," I replied, "you don't ever have to apologize to me for playing poorly. How you play in a game does not in the least affect how I feel about you."

I went on to explain that I was not disappointed in him. I was sad because I knew he was disappointed. However, this was not something he should ever apologize to me for. My love and pride in him had nothing to do with how he played ball. I was proud of him because he's mine. I was excited when he played well, but it did not affect my love for him. I would love and accept him whether he scored twenty points or sat on the bench.

All of us are driven by the desire for acceptance. We want our husbands' acceptance of how we look, how we keep house, and how we raise the children. We want our friends' acceptance and we want our parents' acceptance. There is a basic human need in each of us for acceptance.

A home that is lacking in acceptance is a home where tension, nervousness, and fear control the atmosphere. The family members are uneasy and insecure. A lack of acceptance may be caused by unrealistic expectations that cannot be fulfilled by a family member. There becomes a futile sense that I will never be able to please my spouse or my parents.

In the world, a person's value is often determined by his production or her success. In contrast our homes should offer us a sanctuary of acceptance just as we are. Our acceptance as valuable people is not dependent on our performance, but on the fact

that God made us and loves us. He has placed us in our particular
family.

In first understanding God's acceptance of us, we will gain
insight into our own value and be enabled to be more accepting of
others. There is no way that we can earn God's favor. As Paul
writes to the churches at Ephesus and Rome:

> For by grace you have been saved through faith; and that not of
> yourselves, it is the gift of God; not as a result of works, that no one
> should boast (Ephesians 2:8-9).

> For all have sinned and fall short of the glory of God, being justified
> as a gift by His grace through the redemption which is in Christ
> Jesus (Romans 3:23-24).

In a conversation with a friend who was considering the
Christian faith, two common questions arose. First, she did not
feel she was good enough for God to accept her. In addition, if she
ever did make a commitment to Christ, she was afraid that she
would not be able to "keep it."

Not one of us will ever be good enough for God to accept. We
cannot wait until we straighten out our lives or live up to what we
assume God's expectations of us are because we never will. He
accepts us purely because Jesus died for us. This is His grace—
unconditional love. In accepting His gift of grace we cannot then
expect to be able to "keep it." We will fail and we will sin. For us
He has provided forgiveness. Again, this is His grace—
unconditional acceptance. God accepts us and approves of us
simply because we are His. He does not approve of all of our
behavior. Neither will we approve of the behavior of our children.
Yet we do approve of them as people.

When we have confidence in God's acceptance of us, we will
be more easily able to create an atmosphere of approval and acceptance in our homes. One way in which we communicate acceptance is by showing pride in one another. Mates need to
express pride in each other in front of the children.

I have a vivid mental picture of my own father throwing his
arms around my mother and saying, "You are the best wife I've
ever had." Of course, he only had one! As a child I thought it was
silly, but, oh, how good it made me feel. My dad always built my
mother up, and consequently each of her children valued her gifts
as well.

We also need to commend our children for the unique qualities God has given them. One of my daughters has unusual leadership gifts. This gift sometimes gets her into trouble when it expresses itself in bossiness, yet as she learns how to use this gift, it will be a blessing to many. After an unpleasant episode where she had to be disciplined for giving everyone in the family orders, we had a talk. I shared with her how special she was, and how proud I was of the unusual gift of leadership God had given her. She is young, and she doesn't yet know how to use her gift in a positive manner. I promised her we would work on learning how to use this gift for good and that God would help her.

Supporting our children by being with them in their activities is another way of commending them. Going to that piano recital, that soccer game, or that choir festival illustrates to them that we are proud of them. In creating an atmosphere of love, it is also crucial that we encourage our children to take pride in one another. This means going to each other's events.

Ordinarily, it's the youngest children who get dragged to the older ones' ballgames and performances. By the time the young ones get involved, it's easy for the big kids to be off on their own activities. But older children should be encouraged to be present at some of the younger ones' activities. This visible expression of pride in a younger brother or sister does much to build family unity and acceptance.

Our elementary school has a big music program each spring. All of the young children participate, and they practice for weeks. We calculated that this spring was our tenth elementary school music show to attend. Neither Johnny nor I nor the three big kids wanted to go again. Yet the twins were in it, so we all went, and the boys took their sisters flowers. It was special for the girls to have fans watch them, and it was good for the older children to learn that they too must show pride in their younger sisters.

We have a favorite rendition of spin the bottle. In this game one family member spins a bottle until it stops to point to another person. The spinner then tells this person something he loves about that person. That person then takes the next turn spinning. John says he loves Allison because she helps him with his homework. Libby loves Chris because he shares his gum. This simple game has been a great vehicle for communicating approval in one another and hence building up self-worth.

Negative character assaults should not be permitted in a home where we are seeking to build an atmosphere of acceptance. "You are stupid" is a phrase that we should never permit our children to say to one another. They will naturally try to do it, but we must have the expectation that the children treat each other with respect. This will take training and discipline, but it is important. "Shut up" and "dummy" are typical things children will say to one another that are unkind assaults. If our homes are to be a place where we get filled up with approval to go out into a difficult world, negative put-downs must be eliminated from the beginning.

When I was small, my father used to say to me, "Susan, I am so proud of you." "Why?" I would ask. "Because you are mine" was his reply. Knowing that God accepts us simply because we are His gives us security. Understanding that there is total acceptance of us by our families because we are family will create an atmosphere of approval and a sense of family identity.

A home whose atmosphere is marked by the ingredient of love will be a home where the members sense acceptance from one another, a home where they return to be filled up to go out into the world.

Love Is Appreciation

I walked into the kitchen early one morning to fix breakfast for a hungry crowd. As I turned on the lights I saw dirty dishes where the night before I was sure that I had left things clean. Oh, I groaned inwardly, those "late-night snacks!" "A mother's work is never done," I said in jest to my son who was also gazing at the mess.

"Ahhh," he replied with a twinkle in his eye, "but Mom, you do it so well!" His humorous appreciation of my work was a great beginning to my day. Acceptance is important because it enables us to recognize that a person is valuable just because he is created by God. Acceptance says, "I love you because you are." Appreciation is vital because it allows us to commend what one does. Appreciation says, "I am thankful for what you do." Both traits are important ingredients in building an atmosphere of love.

Failure to be appreciated contributes to the diminishing self-image of the busy mother. Because her tasks are considered "her job" and she is expected to do them, appreciation is seen as unnecessary. Unconsciously, we often slip into the mentality in our homes that if the family member is simply doing his job—for example, making his bed, taking out the trash, fixing a broken cabinet—then appreciation is unnecessary. We fall into the trap of appreciating only those things which are considered "extra."

Even when we or our mates or one of our children completes a regular task that he is expected to do, we should openly appreciate it anyway. Expecting certain standards of behavior, then appreciating the results, do not work at cross purposes. Rather they become mutually beneficial. I expect my sons to routinely take out the trash without complaining. Yet it also encourages them when I remember to thank them for doing it. I expect my children to have friendly manners on the phone. Complimenting them on their manners reinforces the behavior. It is important to expect good standards, and it helps to appreciate the efforts that go into meeting them. We all need to be appreciated for the regular, ordinary things we do.

In Paul we find a person who understood the importance of appreciation. As he wrote to his fellow believers, he continually appreciated them and gave thanks for their faith and encouragement.

First and Second Thessalonians are examples of Paul's expressing appreciation to his friends. "We give thanks to God always for all of you, making mention of you in our prayers" (1 Thessalonians 1:2). "We ought always to give thanks to God for you, brethren, as is only fitting, because your faith is greatly enlarged, and the love of each one of you toward one another grows ever greater" (2 Thessalonians 1:3).

In many of his letters, Paul offered thanksgiving to God for different qualities in the lives of his friends. He also told them how he appreciated the different things that they did. In Paul we see an example of someone who genuinely appreciated others.

As we consider how to help our family cultivate this trait, we can learn from Paul the value of first appreciating God for what He has done. When we develop the habit of thanksgiving in our own prayer life, the joy that this brings our spirit will overflow into our homes. In seeking to cultivate our first priority—that of loving Christ—we will be encouraged when we spend frequent time in prayer giving thanks to God for the things He has done. When we spend time privately thanking God, as we talk with our children, it will be natural to point out to them the many things that we are thankful for.

The diversity of God's creation offers a wealth of things to be thankful for. "Look at the leaves. Isn't God good to make so many different colors? Honey, feel this rock, this moss, this dirt, and this smooth leaf. What do you notice about them? Isn't God good to make things that feel so different to touch? Do you see the tall tree, the tiny mushroom, the big sun? God made so many different sizes. Wouldn't it be sad if everything were the same size?"

"Libby, even though you are twins, you and Susy are different. John and Chris are different, too. No one person is exactly like anyone else. Isn't it amazing how God can make all these different people. I would think He would run out of ideas. Your being different is so special. It makes you extra special to God. Let's thank God for making you special."

Appreciating the things that God has made with our small children will restore to us and instill in them the sense of awe in God's power that we too often take for granted.

Creating a special moment that comes to symbolize appreciating God is helpful in teaching thanksgiving. When Allison was a toddler, we spent vacations on a family farm. Overlooking a grassy field was a large hammock strung between two trees. We loved to curl up together in this hammock. As we swung, we made up a song that we would sing together. "Thank you, Lord, for..." was the complete song. Each of us would take turns filling in the blank. This became our special place of thanksgiving. Whenever I see a hammock it reminds me of those precious moments.

Thanking God in our own prayer lives and creatively helping our children grow in thanking God will open the way for it to become more natural to appreciate each other.

In our marriages, it is easy to become so concerned about our own "rights" that we fail to appreciate one another and we begin to take one another for granted. We constantly need to be thanking each other and saying in front of our children how we appreciate specific things about our mates. It means a lot to a mom when the dad says, "Honey, I appreciate your carpooling the kids all over town today." Mom says, "I appreciate your working hard to provide for us, even when some days you would rather stay in bed."

Don't use phony flattery. Think of the real things you appreciate and say them, and your children will catch the spirit of appreciation. Appreciate and thank your children for little things they say and do. Teach them to thank each other as well.

In family prayer times, it's fun to take turns thanking God for something special that a family member has done. Often we go around in a circle and each person expresses appreciation to God for something about the person on his right. The little ones love it when I write notes on their napkins and hide them in their lunches. Usually I write something simple about why I'm thankful for them, like their warm smile or their happy nature. Leaving periodic notes to each family member expressing praise and appreciation will uplift the person and will help prevent us from taking one another for granted.

Training in manners is a natural way to encourage appreciation as well as respect. Politeness is a sign of respect. Like the quality of sacrifice, the teaching of polite manners is in danger of fading away. We must re-emphasize this with our children. Writing thank-you notes is an unpleasant but vital task for everyone. As soon as our children can write they should learn to send their own child-sized thank yous to special people. Teaching our children to express thanks to the carpool driver, the grandmother, the hostess, and, yes, even their parents and siblings is a crucial step in teaching them the value of appreciation. As we thank others, we are contributing to the building up of their self-worth. Perhaps we need to ask if there is someone today whom we need to call or write to express appreciation.

We can never appreciate our mates or our children too much. It is difficult to overdo appreciation. A home whose atmosphere is marked by the ingredient of love will be a home where the members are continually appreciating one another.

Sacrifice, acceptance, and appreciation will all contribute to creating an atmosphere marked by the ingredient of love.

Forgiveness

The second ingredient reflecting the presence of Christ in the atmosphere of our homes must be the ingredient of forgiveness.

A friend of mine has two toddlers and a brand new baby. One Saturday when she knew her husband could be at home to watch the three boys, she made an appointment to have her hair cut. Not only was she in need of a haircut, but she also needed a few hours away from the children. At the last moment her husband decided to run errands that made him late arriving home to baby-sit. In her disappointment she got angry and when finally he came home, she blew up and stormed angrily out of the house. A cloud of tension settled over the home permeating the atmosphere. By evening she could stand it no longer.

"Honey," she said, "I was wrong to say what I did. Will you forgive me?"

"Yes," he replied, "and will you forgive me for not being sensitive to your need to keep that appointment?"

The tension lifted and through forgiveness, an atmosphere of peace was once again possible. Unless forgiveness is freely flowing in our homes, an atmosphere of bitterness will creep in.

It is difficult to practice forgiveness in our homes unless we first accept God's forgiveness of ourselves. Not only is God's acceptance freely given, but also his forgiveness is always abundant. In order to receive God's forgiveness we must admit our sin and accept Christ's personal death as payment for our sin. Then we can go in confidence to God to ask and to receive His forgiveness. As we experience God's forgiveness in our own lives, we will be enabled to forgive others.

The Bible is an anthology of forgiven men and women. David, the greatest of Israel's kings, committed murder and adultery. Yet he realized what he had done and was devastated by it. In Psalm 51 we see an example of David's broken heart and repentant spirit.

> Be gracious to me, O God,
>   according to Thy lovingkindness;
> According to the greatness of Thy compassion,
>   blot out my transgressions.
> Wash me thoroughly from my iniquity,
>   and cleanse me from my sin.
> For I know my transgressions,
>   and my sin is ever before me.

Luke tells the story of an immoral woman who washed Jesus' feet with her tears, wiping them with her hair and anointing them with perfume. Some of the men who saw her do this were very upset that Jesus would associate with such a sinner. He, however, sensing that what she needed was forgiveness, forgave her of her sins and sent her away in peace.

In the last hour of His life, while in extreme pain as He hung dying on the cross, Jesus gazed out at those responsible for His death. Turning His eyes toward heaven, He prayed, "Father, forgive them; for they do not know what they are doing" (Luke 23:34).

We need the confidence to know that we can always come to God for forgiveness. Sometimes pride gets in the way, and we subtly think we must get our lives in order before we go to God. This implies that we actually believe we'll get our lives in order eventually, and we will be worthy to go to God. It will never happen. God desires for us to come to Him just as we are with all our failures. His forgiveness is always available, but we have to ask for it. When God forgives us, He forgets, and He no longer even remembers our sin. He doesn't keep a record of all of our sins!

As we experience God's forgiveness in our own lives, we will be better able to forgive others. In learning to forgive and to be forgiven in our families, we will be able to cultivate an atmosphere where the aroma of Christ permeates our homes. How does this work out practically in our homes?

Personal Forgiveness

My first responsibility is for my own relationship with God. Seeking His forgiveness for my own wrongs will be a regular part of my time alone with God. Mothers surrounded by small children often suffer from bad attitudes that need to be confessed and forgiven if the atmosphere in the home is to be happy and uplifting.

Perhaps it's resentment at yet another day ahead of being cooped up all alone with small children. Maybe it's bitterness toward a friend who you feel has not paid enough attention to you. Or possibly there is jealousy of someone who you think has everything that you lack. All of these attitudes are common, and they are all sin. When we do not deal with these attitudes, we become critical, bitter women, and the atmosphere in our homes will be a negative one.

Many times I have had to go to God and say, "Lord, I have a

bad attitude about this situation or this person. I know it is wrong and I confess it as sin. Please forgive me and change my attitude."

Not only does God forgive, but He does bring about change as we allow Him to. After receiving forgiveness, we must turn our backs on the sin and move forward into a new day.

Sometimes we have a bad attitude about ourselves. Perhaps we are not happy with how we look, or how we handle our children or run our homes. Self-pity is sin in disguise. It's sin because we are focused on ourselves. The cure is the same. Ask God's forgiveness, then begin to think about how we can be a blessing to others. As we face the sin in our own lives and seek God's forgiveness, we will be enabled to help forgiveness become a natural part of family living.

Forgiving Others

When we begin to experience personal forgiveness, we will be better able to forgive others. Sometimes we don't feel forgiving to our mate or child, but forgiveness does not have a thing to do with feelings. We forgive because God has told us to. Forgiveness must occur before healing can take place. The feelings may still be resentment, yet forgive we must. As the healing begins, the feelings will slowly change, but that may take time.

Recently in a fit of exhaustion and resentment, I lashed out at one of my twins. I also disciplined her unfairly. What she had done was not a big thing, yet in my own state of exhaustion and frustration I had overreacted. After we both calmed down, I went to her and said, "Honey, I was wrong in how I just treated you. You were wrong in what you did, but I overreacted and I should not have treated you the way I did. Will you forgive me?"

"Y-yes," she managed through her tears. Then I prayed with her asking God to forgive me for mistreating her and thanking Him for His forgiveness. Our relationship was restored, and we were able to begin anew. Forgiveness allows relationships to be restored.

Several weeks ago we went on a family hike. Susy was taking her turn as hike leader when she tripped and fell. She was not badly hurt, but one of the boys burst out laughing, and she immediately began to cry. I took my son aside and told him that he must apologize to her and ask her forgiveness. She could have hurt herself and what she needed was a brother to help her rather than laugh at her. She was angry and hurt by his response.

He did not want to apologize or to ask forgiveness. There was a barrier in their relationship that needed to be lifted. The relationship was more important than the incident. We told him he must ask her forgiveness. Finally, under protest he did, and their relationship was restored. As the children learn to ask forgiveness from one another, they are receiving good training for marriage.

Recently I opened my front door to find a small seven-year-old with tears streaming down her face.

"What in the world is the matter," I asked my young friend.

"Oh," she sobbed, "I have been so mean to my mother and said such ugly things to her."

I took her onto my lap and told her about God and His forgiveness. I asked her if she wanted God to forgive her and she said "yes." So we prayed for forgiveness, and He did forgive her. I then suggested that it might be nice if she wrote her mother a note saying how sorry she was and asking her to forgive her for talking ugly. After the note was finished she went off happily to play with the other children. In each of us, children and adults, there is an inherent need to forgive and to be forgiven.

Perhaps love and forgiveness were missing from your home when you were a child. Possibly divorce, alcoholism, or even abuse was present instead. It is important not to let the past control you. The key to this is forgiveness. We must forgive our parents and look to God to begin healing us. Spending time with a few close Christian friends for encouragement will help in this process of healing. Reading good books on the family will help also. In addition, seek out an older couple as a model to adopt as "grandparents." They will be a tremendous source of wisdom and comfort. We will discover that as we seek to forgive those who have let us down in the past, an atmosphere of forgiveness will begin to permeate our own homes.

Believing the Best

Forgiveness in a sense is a beginning. Forgiveness between two people or between one person and God ushers in a new relationship. The first time we ask forgiveness will be the hardest. Once we experience the healing that forgiveness brings, we will be so glad we sought forgiveness. Confessing our sins and asking forgiveness will never be pleasant or natural. We will usually do it out of conviction rather than feeling.

Accompanying forgiveness should be hope. Included in the well-known passage on love found in 1 Corinthians 13 is the phrase "love bears all things, believes all things, and hopes all things." Hope and faith in God's changing power enables us to believe the best about ourselves and others. Because of God's power we can count on Him not only to forgive us but to begin to change us and to change others. When we are discouraged, we need to see forgiveness as a new beginning, then to eagerly await the miracle of change that God will bring about as we allow Him to work in our lives.

When forgiveness and hope are ingredients in the atmosphere of a home, laughter, and joy will naturally result.

Joy

Little John had the flu; Susy, a bladder infection; Allison, bad allergies; Chris was jealous that John was sick so he declared that he had a tummy ache; and Dad had a sore throat! Libby had a nose that ran into her food. At least I did not have "morning sickness"!

It was bitterly cold and grey outdoors so I tried to build a fire. Alas, the vent did not work. The house filled with smoke setting off a very loud smoke alarm that frightened the babies, who began to scream. It took me ten minutes to unhitch the smoke alarm as the battery was stuck. Finally the noise stopped, and I rushed to open windows to clear the house of smoke.

Meanwhile, Libby found the Elmer's glue I was sure was out of reach and covered herself and the easy chair. Susy climbed on top of my desk to color my checkbook with an orange magic marker. John stomped around the living room stark naked claiming that he didn't need a bath even though it had been three days. I said he did. He said it was his body! We all laughed. It was just a typical day in the Yates household.

In homes where small children reign, the normal chaos of busy toddlers often produces either tears or laughter in their moms. We may find ourselves simply trying to endure the season rather than enjoying it. God, however, has more for us than pure endurance. He has a deep joy that He wishes for us to experience—joy in His presence, joy in our situations, and joy in our young families. How then can we experience this supernatural joy in a home that often seems beyond control?

The joy that God has for us and for the atmosphere in our homes is both supernatural and refreshing. Supernatural joy is based on our relationship with Christ. When we come to God asking forgiveness of our sins and seeking a relationship with Him through Christ, we bring great joy to our Heavenly Father. Indeed, we have been compared to a lost sheep that has strayed away and finally been found by its shepherd. As Luke 15:7 says, "There will be more joy in heaven over one sinner who repents, than over ninety-nine righteous persons who need no repentance." It is a bit overwhelming to think that we bring God joy.

This supernatural joy that God desires for us to experience is distinct from happiness. Happiness is usually caused by circumstances. When things are going great, we feel happy; when life is unpleasant, we are depressed. Supernatural joy, however, enables us to experience a deeper joy that is not so dependent on our circumstances. As we live by correct priorities, cultivating our relationship with Christ on a daily basis, we will begin to experience a quiet joy resulting from a sense of security that we belong to God, and He is indeed in control of our lives.

When we focus on this security, we will be free to relax and trust Him in whatever situation we find ourselves. We will not always feel happy, but we will have a deeper sense of joy that we belong to Christ and that His plans for us are good. God's joy is supernatural.

His joy is also refreshing. Here are three aspects to that joy.

Praise Produces Joy

Jim Houston once said God has not called us to a life of obligation but to a life of gratitude. So often busy mothers are overwhelmed with obligations. There are so many small voices calling out for mama. It is easy to be overcome by the demands upon us, and in struggling to fulfill our obligation we often become frustrated or depressed. We forget to have hearts of gratitude.

To experience the refreshment that joy can bring, we must become mothers who praise. I am not a morning person, and I hate to get up. However, when I take a few minutes early in the morning before I even get out of bed to praise God, I find that I enter into the day with a positive attitude rather than a negative one. There are at least two types of praise: thanking God for who He is and praising Him for what He has done.

"Lord, thank you that you are all powerful. When the world and my household seem chaotic, you are still in charge. You know each of my children. You made them. You alone are perfect love. You love my children even more than I do. Your goodness is overwhelming. Thank you, Lord."

"Thank you, Lord, for what you have done. You have given me these children. They are healthy. You have given me a husband who loves his family. You have provided for all of our real needs. Thank you, Lord."

Praise refreshes us. Cultivating the habit of praising God also makes it more natural for us to praise one another in the family. "Honey, you are such a good father." Or, "Son, you did a great job today reading to me from that difficult book." Praise and appreciation are similar qualities in a home marked by an atmosphere of joy.

A Positive Spirit Cultivates Joy

Some people come into the world with a positive nature. They always seem to be able to see the bright side of things. Others look at a situation and immediately see all of the negatives. We may have one family member who is constantly negative. It can be very aggravating to live with a negative mate or child.

It is possible to begin to cultivate a positive nature in those for whom this is not natural. Joy will be the result. In cultivating a positive spirit, it is helpful to take time each day for prayers of praise and thanksgiving. The evening meal might be an appropriate time for each person to pray thanking God for something special that He has done that day.

It is helpful as well to ask ourselves what it is that we think about. Paul recommends, "Whatever is true, whatever is honorable, whatever is right, whatever is pure, whatever is lovely, whatever is of good repute, if there is any excellence and if anything worthy of praise, let your mind dwell on these things" (Philippians 4:8). Where our mind is will determine in part whether we are a joyful person or one who frequently complains.

Discussing good things as a family will also aid in cultivating a positive spirit. "What did you enjoy the most at school today?" Or "What are your favorite toys?" Or "What book do you like the best?" When we discuss things and people whom we enjoy, we begin to train ourselves in appreciating the good around us rather than focusing on things to complain about.

When we are faced with an unpleasant situation, we need to have an attitude of expectancy. As we expect to learn something valuable in unpleasant circumstances, the situation will at least have a productive outcome. As parents we should be praying for God to cultivate a positive spirit in each of our children and in both of their parents.

Laughter Promotes Joy

Not too long ago we got a new Golden Retriever puppy. Upon seeing the dog, Susy cried out, "But Mommy, I wanted an elephant." Children say the funniest things, and they naturally bring humor into young families. One of the greatest medicines in the world is laughter. In our homes we desperately need to laugh.

One of the qualities I pray for regularly in my children is that they have a sense of humor. Laughter can cover a multitude of mistakes. It can ease the pain of many failures, and it can cut through a tense moment turning it from potential hurt and restoring a threatened relationship. A home marked by joy is a home where we learn to laugh at ourselves and our situations. I'm sure that our Heavenly Father has a great sense of humor. How He must chuckle at some of the messes we get ourselves into. We all take ourselves too seriously. Humor can bring perspective back into a situation that has gotten far too serious. To be able to laugh at oneself is a great trait. As we attempt to laugh at ourselves we will create a lightheartedness in the family.

One word of caution is in order, though. Humor that is sarcastic is rarely helpful. Indeed, it can be biting and destructive. There is much that is funny that is wholesome. Sarcasm is not necessary for entertainment.

As moms we need to develop the quality of being able to laugh at our situations. Some people are more naturally gifted with a sense of humor than others. In some it must be cultivated.

Sometimes doing silly skits and playing practical jokes can add a dimension of humor. We have to carefully pick our practical jokes. This year I dressed up in a costume and went to my son's junior high Halloween dance. He didn't recognize me for the longest time, and when one of his girlfriends did, it was so funny. Now I'd never do that to my high schooler. It would embarrass her to death.

Once Johnny and I went disguised as very old people to a retirement party for a close friend. Our kids helped us get ready, and it was a great joke for all.

One April Fool's Day, my husband and I came home from a dinner engagement to find that our children had short-sheeted our bed, put Saran Wrap over our toilet seat, and stockings over our shower nozzle! Loud giggles were heard coming from each of their bedrooms as our shrieks let them know we had fallen for their pranks. As adults we should take care not to lose the sense of fun that children have, and we must be creative in cultivating humor in our homes.

Another key in developing humor lies in keeping our perspective. Something that seems so important right now will often seem irrelevant next month. People's perspectives are so different. Chris once told me that he had found a very valuable antique nickel—made in 1964!

A couple of years ago we went on a trip out West. We met a farmer in a small Kansas town of three hundred. He told us that he had gotten fed up with that town because it was getting too big, so he was moving to the country. On this same trip we took the children to see a replica of a frontier village. They saw demonstrations of women weaving and making pottery. They were so amazed at how hard women had to work back in those days! Being reminded of the many different perspectives people have will help in understanding one another and will provide opportunities for humor.

An atmosphere which is marked by joy will prevail in a home where laughter is frequent.

Our Unique Atmosphere

Friends of ours recently moved to another city. In the process of house hunting, they found two homes that were very different. They liked both of them and could not decide which one was the better. In an effort to decide, they made lists to compare the two homes, but still they were unable to make a decision. Finally, they asked themselves the question, which house will best enable us to create the atmosphere unique to our family? As they discussed what feeling they wanted their home to portray, it became evident to them which home was the right choice. Ann and Doug have special gifts in relating to people. Many people come to their home. Ann's talents in decorating communicate warmth and openness. Both of them share a wonderful sense of humor, and their home is a place of laughter.

As they considered the special nature of their family, they were able to determine which of the two homes would enable their gifts to be used in the best way.

There are no two families which are exactly alike. As individuals we all have different gifts and interests. Thus our families will also have a distinctiveness determined in part by the gifts of the individuals in it. Naturally, we all want love, forgiveness, and joy to permeate our homes. In addition, we want to add our special unique flavor to the atmosphere of our home.

A pleasing atmosphere is not determined by material possessions, financial resources, the number of children, or the size of the home. What we possess is not nearly as important as who we are. Rather a pleasing atmosphere is created as family members seek to grow in love, forgiveness, and joy, and as they encourage each other in sharing their individual talents.

One family may have exceptional musical talents. Singing together around a piano or enjoying playing instruments as a family might be a common occurrence in this home. I love to visit a home where music is an important ingredient. I appreciate it because I have no musical talent. When I sing, my children groan! Musical ability is a special gift that when cultivated will bring much joy not only to the family members but also to those who visit in their musical home.

You may love to read and your home may reflect a quiet, relaxed retreat. Perhaps as a family you enjoy curling up together and reading aloud. Serenity and peace may flavor the atmosphere in your home.

Another family might enjoy board games. Visiting in this home will provide stimulating competition. Another family might be interested in the arts or in sports.

In determining the special flavor we want to permeate our family's atmosphere, we first need to think through the gifts and interests of the family members. As mother and chief architect of the atmosphere in my home, what are my special talents and how can they be used to enhance the atmosphere of our home? What different interests do the other family members have and how can I encourage them to express these in our home?

When our children are small their talents may not be as evident, and the atmosphere will be determined by the interests of the parents. However, as the children develop, their unique gifts when encouraged will enhance the atmosphere in our homes.

Love, forgiveness, and joy are three of the ingredients which will reflect the fragrance of Christ as we develop them in our homes. Our unique families will add a special flavor to the atmosphere. A home where the fragrance of Christ is present will be a home that provides comfort and shelter from the world. It will be a home that also equips its members to go out, filled and recharged with a message of love to a needy world.

Focus Questions

Meditate on Romans 12.

1. What qualities are found here that I would want to characterize the atmosphere of my home?
2. What are small steps that I can take this week to help love, joy, and forgiveness grow in my home?
3. What are the unique gifts and interests of my family? How can I help them creatively enhance the atmosphere in our home?

Write a prayer for the atmosphere in your home based on your study of Romans 12.

EIGHT

FINDING GOOD ROLE MODELS FOR OUR FAMILIES

A quick glance into the refrigerator told me the bad news: I was out of milk again. I'm sure, I mused, that we have a food monster whose main aim and ambition in life is to frustrate me. He sneaks into the kitchen when I am not looking and eats only those basic items I'm sure I have plenty of. He regularly devours my milk, bread, and peanut butter right before I need them to feed hungry toddlers.

With a sigh of despair, I went to find four small children for another trip to the grocery store. I found three children fairly quickly, but Susy was missing. No one seemed to know where she was.

"Oh, no, she's in trouble," I thought with a flash of panic. Then I saw it—a trail of clothes. First, it was the pink sunsuit I had put on her that morning. A little further along the hall was a sock, then panties, and a shoe. The clothes trail led me straight to Christopher's closet where I found a happy three-year-old struggling into her six-year-old brother's shoes, pants, and shirt.

A huge smile spread across her chubby cheeks as she proudly announced to me, "Mama, I'm a pretend boy."

The battle to make her change clothes was not worth the effort, so off we went to the store with two real boys, one small twin girl and her "pretend twin brother." Although they are not identical, the girls look very much alike, so often people will stop them to ask if they are twins. On this particular day, a lovely lady, elegantly dressed for some special occasion, approached my ragged looking group and politely remarked to the girls, "You girls are so cute. Are you twins?" Susy, thoroughly exasperated, looked her straight in the eye as she replied, "No, I'm a boy."

For several more days Susy dressed in Christopher's clothes whenever she could. She delighted in telling people that she was a boy. At a meeting in our home the children took turns introducing themselves. When Susy's turn came, she proudly stood and said, "My name is George."

Her fantasy with wanting to be just like her older brother did not last long. The girls soon switched to dressing up like "big ladies" in some of mom's old clothes. One day as I worked close by, I listened to the talk between three-year-old girls playing big ladies.

"Libby, you take the carpool while I go play tennis," Susy ordered.

With her hand on her hip in a frustrated pose, Libby replied, "Susy, you will just have to manage. I'm going out."

Children love to pretend to be other people. Pretending to be nurses, soldiers, teachers, policemen, or even brothers, they delight in copying the people that they admire. They imitate the voices, the movements, and the appearances.

At the earliest age, the primary source of role models for small children is family members. Our infants learn to "coo" as they hear us coo. They learn to clap as we clap; and as they begin to talk, they even say some of the same things they've heard us say.

In their play, little children often pretend to be Mommy and Daddy. My five-year-old niece, whose father is an accountant, was playing with her younger sister in the backyard. As they counted the green leaves that were money, she was overheard to say, "Oh, my, I have to work so hard because it's tax season."

She did not have any idea what taxes were, but she was happily imitating what she heard discussed by her parents.

When our children are small and the greatest influence is that of the parents, brothers, and sisters, we are not as concerned with the question of role models for them. At this age we have a greater degree of control over the influences in their lives.

The beginning of school, however, ushers in a new season in role models. Increased exposure to other children and adults combined with a growing tendency to relate to their peers provides more opportunity for role models outside the family.

Many of these new influences can be good. Some, however, will be disappointing. A six-year-old may come home with a new vocabulary of bad words he has learned from his classmate. An eight-year-old may be in tears because the teacher whom she admired lost her temper and yelled at her. The young teenager may admire an older teenager until he hears that the older one was caught cheating on a test in school.

Not only do our children need good role models, though, we need them, too. Like them, we need to be exposed to other adults whom we admire. We need older Christians that we can look to for encouragement in our faith. We need to know older parents who will be examples for us and who can help us with our questions about raising children.

Without adequate role models, parenting can be a lonely, fearful occupation. We may have a crisis of confidence in raising our children because there seem to be few people to whom we can turn for advice and encouragement. In addition, we may worry because our children don't have the wholesome heroes to look up to that we did when we were young.

How can we find good role models for ourselves and our children? Are there good role models today? How do we learn to deal with disappointment when those whom we admire let us down?

As we look at the world around us, we may be discouraged by the utter dearth of good role models for us as parents and for our children. What has caused this decline of good role models in today's society? There appear to be at least four reasons for this void.

First, the influence of a sophisticated secular media has had a tremendous impact upon each of our lives. We are no longer limited to the printed word and to the radio. We are bombarded by television, movies, tapes, and videos as well as by numerous magazines and books. Unfortunately, many of the celebrities spotlighted in the media are not the sort of people that we would want to emulate or that we would want our children to follow.

Second, because of the increased mobility in our society, many families are living far away from their own relatives. It is no longer common to live up the street from mom and dad. Whereas grandparents, parents, and cousins used to be found living in close proximity, today's families are separated by many miles and contact limited to infrequent visits. The examples and the encouragement from older family members living nearby has become the exception rather than the norm.

A third cause of the decline of good role models can be attributed to the increasing breakup of marriages. Many more children today are being raised by single parents without the benefit of two adult models in the same home. There is an increase in stepparents and stepbrothers and stepsisters. Some children have not had the experience of seeing a marriage that really does work.

A final cause of decreasing positive role models has simply been the unintentional acceptance of this void. Perhaps we have failed to look for and to seek out good role models for our families. Sometimes this has been due to fear. We have seen too many "heroes" fall and let us down, and we become afraid to look up to anyone again. We are no longer willing to put someone on a pedestal for fear that he will not live up to our expectations, and we will once again be disappointed. In addition, we are often fearful of our children idolizing someone, particularly an outspoken believer, because that person may be found to have a lifestyle inconsistent with the Christian values he or she proclaims. When this happens we wonder if there are indeed any believers who practice what they preach.

It is important to distinguish between heroes and role models. Heroes have in the past been associated with hero worship. The dictionary defines hero worship as "to revere as an ideal." Our disappointments in our heroes can come if we worship them as heroes rather than seeing them merely as role models. A role model is "a person with weaknesses and sin just like us." There are no perfect people. In looking to role models as examples, we must realize that the person whom we admire in some areas may be a failure in other areas.

We will all be let down if we worship a person. We are meant to worship God only and to look to good role models as examples. A good role model is someone whom we admire, who because of certain traits in his life encourages us. There are bad role models as well. In essence, everyone is a role model to someone whether he realizes it or not.

We want to learn how to find good examples for ourselves and for our children. We also desire to teach our children how to determine the qualities in people which they should copy and to ignore those weaknesses which they should not. In attempting to find role models for our families, it is helpful to look first to God's Word for some examples.

Three Biblical Role Models

One of the exciting aspects about God's Word is its total realism. It is not a book full of success stories of men and women who put their faith in God and live perfect lives. Rather it is a story of a perfect God at work in the lives of imperfect people—people like you and me who take small steps of faith, then fall down, people who believe God one moment and the next begin to worry. It is indeed the story of God's faithfulness to an unfaithful people. From these lives, though, we can learn much. By studying Biblical characters we catch a glimpse of good role models and bad role models. We are also reminded of God's desires for our lives as we see Him at work in the lives of early believers.

Three diverse role models found in Scripture are Eli, the priest; Peter, the apostle; and Mary, the mother of Jesus.

Eli: Model of a Poor Parent

Eli was a priest at Shiloh. He had two sons, Hophni and Phinehas, who were also priests there. Even though Hophni and Phinehas were priests, they were said to be worthless men who did not even know the Lord. Eli knew about the many evil things that his sons were doing, but according to Scripture, he did not do anything about them or their behavior.

Into this unhappy family came the boy Samuel. Hannah, his mother, had prayed many years for a child, and God had answered her prayer with the gift of Samuel. In thanksgiving, Hannah gave Samuel to the Lord at an early age. This meant that young Samuel went to live with Eli the priest as an adopted son.

As Samuel grew up, he loved God and became a judge over

the children of Israel, and in effect their leader under God. However, Samuel had two sons, Joel and Abijah, who did not follow God but were very wicked. Because Samuel's sons were so bad, the elders of Israel demanded a king to succeed Samuel. This demand was ultimately to bring much sadness to the children of Israel.

It is interesting to look at the impact of Eli's ineffective parenting upon the whole history of Israel. Eli failed to discipline his own sons, and he also failed to be a good role model as a father to Samuel. With no good example to follow himself, Samuel also failed in controlling his sons. From the example of Eli, we can all learn the importance of discipline in raising children.

Was Eli a bad role model? As a parent, yes. As one who loved God, no. The story of Eli serves as a sad model to us of a man who loved God but who neglected to do what he should have done in disciplining his children, and as a result, many suffered.

Peter: Example of Encouragement

Peter, the apostle, is another role model. In Matthew 16, we see one episode in Peter's life as he realized that Jesus was indeed the Christ, the Son of the Living God. We hear Jesus promise Peter that He will use him in a significant role as He builds the church. Surely this must have been a major highlight in Peter's life. Yet it was right after this wonderful affirmation of Peter by Jesus that Peter made a fool of himself.

When told of the suffering that must come to Jesus, Peter said, "God forbid it, Lord! This shall never happen to you" (Matthew 16:22).

Jesus, turning to Peter, replied, "Get behind me, Satan. You are a stumbling block to Me, for you are not setting your mind on God's interests, but man's" (Matthew 16:23).

Poor Peter. How devastated he must have been.

Later, as Christ was about to be crucified, Peter denied three times that he even knew Him—all after promising that he would die himself before he would deny Jesus. As we study the life of Peter, we see an example of a man who truly believed in Jesus, yet we see a man who often failed in living up to his own expectations.

In observing how Jesus dealt with Peter, it becomes clear that

Jesus knew Peter's heart was good. He wanted to do what was right in God's eyes. He often failed, yet he continued to believe and to grow in his faith in Jesus.

It is comforting to look at Peter as a role model. We can identify with him in our enthusiasm to believe. We can identify with him in our failings. We are encouraged as we realize that God uses ordinary human beings like Peter to bring His message to many. If God can use a man who tries to interfere with His will, who even denies Him, then perhaps He can use us with all of our failings. Peter is an example of how God uses human frailty, even in a significant role of building the church. Peter is an example of encouragement.

Mary: Model of One Who Trusted

From Mary, the mother of Jesus, we can learn so many different things. We may identify with her fear as she is approached by the angel Gabriel. How frightened we too would be if suddenly we were face to face with an angel! When he tells her that she will have a son, she asks, "How?" She has a freedom in sharing her questions and fears with God's messenger. We too should have a confidence in talking to God about anything, including our doubts and our fears.

At the end of her conversation with Gabriel, Mary says, "Behold the bondslave of the Lord; be it done to me according to your word" (Luke 1:38). In this statement, Mary is essentially telling God that He may have her life to do with it whatever He desires. What an amazing statement of faith.

For us as women, Mary is a role model of one who gave herself totally to God to be used in whatever way He desired. In so doing, she was privileged to become the mother of our Lord. As we too learn to trust God, we will discover that the plans He has for us are the very best. We can learn much about trust as we look at the life of Mary.

The Scriptures are an excellent beginning in a search for role models. By studying the different characters in the Bible, we are able to see what happens when God's ways are followed and what happens when they are not. Through the lives of many Biblical personalities, we will be encouraged as we see how God has worked in the past in the lives of others. As we look to God's

Word, we will learn what God's values are, and in turn, we will have the basis for our own value system.

In seeking to discover role models for our families, the Bible is a good place to begin. Biblical role models will be an encouragement to us and to our children. Through these stories we become acquainted with people of great faith. In the process we come to know God better as we learn how He interacted with these personalities. In addition to Biblical role models, we also need living examples whose lives we can observe from day to day. Although we appreciate the value of good role models, we sometimes wonder how to determine which people would be good examples. What qualities should we look for in those we wish to follow?

Qualities to Look for in Role Models

There are at least four qualities which every good role model will possess.

First, because we desire to have a family whose members are growing in their faith in Christ, we will naturally look to people who themselves have a strong faith. When as a mother I worry about one of my children, I long for the encouragement of another mother who will not only give me practical advice, but who will also encourage me to trust God with the problem. It is wonderful to be able to share a family need with a friend and to have her pray with you about your concern. When the solutions to the problems and answers to questions do not come quickly, it is a blessing to have another adult who, in praying for you, reminds you of God's concern and of His faithfulness.

Our children also need role models with a deep faith in Christ. When one of my boys was eight, he began to worry about many things. His imagination was overactive, and he was needlessly worrying about things over which he had no control. I tried to comfort him, but alas, my encouragement was not enough. His older sister, however, had had a similar experience a few years earlier, so I asked her to talk with him. Not only did she share her experiences with him, but she also prayed with him about his concern. Her faith was a living example to him. Her counsel comforted him and encouraged his faith to grow when in praying together they sought God's help with his problem. As families desiring to grow in trusting God, we want role models who have a faith that will encourage our faith.

Wisdom is a second quality that we should look for in a good role model. We will often find ourselves in situations with our marriages or with our children that we just don't know how to handle. I recently found myself in a difficult situation with my seven-year-old twins which I did not know how to handle. One of their school teachers called to tell me that she was having trouble with the girls because they were being clique-ish and leaving other children out. A friend in my neighborhood had also watched as they chose one small girl to play with and intentionally left out another who ran home in tears. When my older children had been through this common stage, we had talked with them and their behavior had improved. However, with the twins, talk had not helped the situation. I had done my best to explain to them how it hurt to be left out and that they must not do this to other children. They listened, then went out and did it again! I was completely baffled and did not know what to do. I lacked the wisdom to handle this situation.

I picked up the telephone and called my mother. A strong believer, former school teacher, and mother of four, she had always been to me a reservoir of wisdom. It was natural once again to call her for advice.

"Susan," she said, "the problem is that when you discuss feeling left out, the twins cannot relate to what you are saying. Because they always have each other and are best friends, they have never experienced the pain of exclusion. Therefore, they do not realize the hurt they are causing other children when they leave them out."

Immediately, I realized that my mother was right, and we began to think of creative ways in which we could help the twins understand the pain of exclusion. Being able to benefit from the wisdom of my mother has been an encouragement to me. As mothers, we will all have situations which stump us, and we need other women whose wisdom we can call on.

A third quality that a good role model will possess is experience. Wisdom and experience are closely related. It is in the experiences of parenting that we acquire wisdom. Some new parents will have an unusual gift of wisdom, but most likely those with more experience will be the greatest help to us.

One young mother, Teresa, was having trouble with her two-and-a-half-year-old daughter Katie's adjustment to a new sister. The toddler demanded continual attention and did not like it when her mother had to care for the baby. Whenever Teresa would nurse the baby, Katie would misbehave. A friend who had experienced a similar situation with her children was able to offer some advice. First, she reassured Teresa that Katie's jealousy was a normal occurrence. Then she suggested that whenever Teresa nursed the baby that she have Katie get one of her dolls and pretend to nurse her. As they sat side by side, Teresa could point out to Katie how much fun it was that they could take care of their "babies" together. It was a good time for Teresa to tell Katie how proud she was of her, proud that she was a big sister, proud that she was learning to be patient while Mommy fed the baby, and proud that she was learning to be a helper.

The "school" for mothers is experience, and phoning our friends who have "graduated" from toddler classes can supply us with a wealth of ideas.

Recently, a young girl in our neighborhood came to talk to my daughter Allison about a problem she was having with her best friend. The neighbor is three years younger than my daughter. Her best friend had begun to ignore her and spend time with a group of kids with questionable values. In consoling her, Allison said, "I remember the same thing happening to me, and it used to put me in tears. I finally realized that my friend might eventually change her ways and reevaluate her new friendships. Meanwhile, you must be patient and love her and pray for her."

The comfort for my young neighbor came in talking to someone older who had experienced a similar problem.

Objectivity is a fourth trait to consider in a positive role model. Our tendency as parents in dealing with our own mates and children is to be subjective. It is difficult to separate ourselves from the emotional involvement with our children. A situation may overwhelm us, and we do not seem to be able to see things clearly. The objective advice of someone we admire often brings clarity to a confused situation.

A friend of mine was concerned about her seven-year-old son.

She feared that socially he was not developing as he ought to. He did not seem to have a best friend, and she worried that he was not relating to his peers as he should. She made a wise decision to talk to his teacher. The teacher was able to be more objective. She saw the child in a situation outside the home. She felt that he was very well adjusted and got along well with other boys in his class. The teacher reassured the mother and put her mind at ease.

A new mother was horrified when she had trouble with her two-year-old daughter biting. Even her mother-in-law was afraid that they had a terrible problem within the family. With firm parental discipline, the child soon learned that her behavior was unacceptable, and the parents realized that this problem was typical of two-year-olds. Now this child has a baby brother and when he bites, his big four-year-old sister says, "Oh, he's going through a stage. He will get better."

Objectivity enables a huge problem to become a more manageable one. Objectivity comes as we put some distance between ourselves and the issue. Parents of teens are able to be more objective about the trials of raising toddlers. They can give us good advice because they are somewhat removed from that season. A strong faith, wisdom, experience, and objectivity are four traits that we should seek in others as we look to them for advice.

In addition, it is important that we gain a proper perspective on role models in order to avoid the pitfalls of hero worship. How do we maintain this proper perspective and, even more importantly, how do we help our children learn to benefit from role models while at the same time avoiding hero worship?

A Proper Perspective on Role Models

Drawing the distinction between admiring qualities and gifts in role models while recognizing weaknesses is necessary to avoid hero worship. There will rarely be one person whom we want to totally emulate. There may be someone whose advice you would seek about parenting but not about finances. Another friend may have gifts in the area of homemaking and hospitality, but you would not want her counsel on a marital difficulty. It is easier for adults to make these distinctions than for young children.

A seven-year-old may try to copy his friend who is the best athlete in the class. The athlete may also be a discipline problem, speaking rudely to the teachers and not following instructions. We are thankful that our son works hard to excel in sports, but we worry as we see him also picking up the rudeness of his friend.

It is necessary that we help our children distinguish between these different qualities in individuals, then choose the good qualities to copy. Helping our children acquire a healthy perspective on role models is a gradual process with at least four aspects.

Shared values is the first aspect in developing a proper perspective on role models. Our values give us the foundation from which we are able to distinguish the good qualities from the bad qualities. Our children will understand many of our values simply by living in close proximity with us. They will know instinctively what we approve of and what displeases us. In addition, they will learn what we believe and why as we talk with them.

A mother of a two- or three-year-old can become frustrated with all the "whys" that are thrown at her when she makes a request. "Son, it's time to go to bed now."

"Why, Mommy?"

"Because it's late and you need your sleep."

"I'm not tired. Why do I have to go to bed?"

"Why, why?"

And on goes the battle until the frustrated mother says, "Because I said so!"

Our children must learn that they often have to do things simply because we say so. On the other hand, it is helpful to explain the reasons for our decisions as much as possible. As our children begin to grow up, it will become easier to share with them why we believe and behave the way we do.

When I was young, I took some colorful rubber bands from the local stationery store. In the car on the way home, my parents asked me what I was hiding in my pocket. After much persuasion, I produced my new "toy." My parents explained to me that what I had done was wrong. It was called stealing, and we did not do this in our family. Back to the store we went where I had to apologize to the manager and return the rubber bands. I was a very embarrassed little girl. Quickly, I had learned that honesty had a high value in our home.

Spending time with our children doing ordinary things provides many opportunities for communicating values. Sometimes we communicate our faults as well. The flashing blue lights appeared in my rear view mirror, and the siren broke into the chattering voices of young children. I sighed as I pulled over to the side of the highway. It was the eleventh hour of a twelve-hour car trip with five children by myself. I was ready to get home, and I knew I was going too fast.

"Ma'am, do you know that you were speeding back there?" the officer said in a firm voice as I rolled down my window. "Yes, I'm sorry, I know that I was."

As he proceeded to lecture me and to write me out a ticket, there was dead silence from the back seat. When he had finished, he said, "Ma'am, please drive slowly. You have a precious cargo."

"I know. You're right. And thanks," I replied.

As we pulled out to start the last hour of the trip, one of my children said, "That bum, he should not have done that. You weren't doing anything wrong."

"Now wait a minute," I replied. "I was wrong. I was going too fast. He was right to give me a ticket. He was doing his job. I have to learn to drive slower."

My children did not want their mother to be in trouble, but she was, and she deserved it!

Admitting our own failings to our children will help keep them from unrealistically worshiping us. Acknowledging our mistakes will also make it easier for our children to admit their failures as they grow up. They will see us fail. They need to see us be honest about our failures and to watch as we attempt to make restitution. Our values will be communicated to our children as they see us handle difficult situations.

A second aspect in helping our children become aware of good qualities to emulate in people involves emphasizing the good traits which we observe in others.

My station wagon was packed with five squirming six-year-old boys all talking at once about their baseball practice. The boys hardly noticed that I was there as they each gave their opinions on the new coach and on who was the best batter. Doors slammed shut as I let the children out in front of each of their homes. During the entire ride, only one boy in the car spoke to me. When we reached his house, John David said, "Thank you for the ride, Mrs. Yates."

At the dinner table that evening, I discussed the carpool with my children and told them how impressed I was with John David's manners. It was not the first time we would applaud his manners. All of the children in his family had beautiful manners, and they have become an example to our family.

When our children were small, a mother and daughter used to babysit for us. The father in the family had died at a young age of a heart attack. The family had little money, but they always brought my children the loveliest gifts. Their generosity has overwhelmed us. We have often discussed their unusual gift of giving with our children. Generosity is a wonderful trait to emulate.

I have learned much about human relations and respect for all people from shopping with my mother-in-law. She is a dignified southern lady. Over the years I have watched as she relates to store clerks, postal workers, and gas attendants. Her attitude is beyond polite. She expresses an interest in each person no matter what he does. It is not unusual for her to say to a harassed grocery store clerk, "My, you have the prettiest eyes." On a hot day you might find her fixing a cold drink for the postman to carry on his rounds. She has been a role model to me of one who truly cares for those who serve us. As we emphasize and appreciate the good qualities in people, our children will learn further what traits we desire for them to copy in people.

Teaching our children discernment is a third aspect in maintaining a proper perspective on role models. During the season of toddlers and small children, we have an open window to teach our children our values. Part of teaching values involves training in discernment. Some parents assume that discussions of values are most beneficial when the children become teenagers. Then when we see the bad influences surrounding our teens, we panic and attempt to begin teaching those values we perhaps assumed were being taught when they were young. The window may not be as open to the parents of adolescents. It is crucial that we begin to teach our children discernment from a very young age. In a certain sense, by the time our children become thirteen, much of the teaching-training aspect of parenting is finished. Our role shifts to that of advisor and counselor.

The younger the child, the easier it is to mold and teach them values. They are more receptive to parents at a tender age and do not yet have the experience to present numerous alternatives. In teaching our children God's values, we equip them with a basis for their own values. Studying characters like Peter, Eli, and Mary is one way of opening our children's eyes to the values which God desires for us.

Knowing God's values and the lifestyle He has for us provides the foundation from which to discern what qualities to copy in a role model and which to ignore.

Mark, aged seven, told his mother one day, "Mom, I love rock music."

"Oh," said his mother, "do all your friends like rock music?"

"Oh yes, all but one," replied Mark.

"Mark, do you know what some of the words mean in rock music?" questioned his mom.

"No," he replied.

This mother went on to explain to him some of the phrases in rock music and what they meant. She also discussed with Mark that what God's Word taught was rather different from the phrases he was hearing. "Wow, I bet my friends Peter and Joey don't know that either."

"Mark, it is always important to think about what the words are and to decide if it is good. Let's go and pick out some rock singers who sing about God's love."

"Okay, Mom, and I'll tell Peter and Joey about the good rock and the bad rock."

A teenager may not be as receptive to his parents' critique of his music. However, if he has been taught values and discernment at an early age, he will be more likely to make wise judgments during the teen years. We are surrounded with opportunities to train our children in discernment.

The television hosts a great diversity of role models. One young mother of four was watching a popular educational show with her toddlers. While the puppets taught many good things to the children, she noticed that when the puppets spoke to each other, it was often rude. There was a strong element of sarcasm and an obvious lack of compassion. Sitting in front of the television, she asked her four-year-old, "Is that puppet speaking in a kind way to his friend?"

The child thought for a moment and said, "I guess not."

"How should we speak to each other?" continued the mom. "We should be sweet," answered her child.

Mr. Rogers' "Neighborhood of Make Believe" is a good lesson in teaching discernment. Occasionally, the characters in the Neighborhood of Make Believe do not act kindly toward one another. When the audience returns to Mr. Rogers from the Neighborhood of Make Believe, he asks the children why the characters were behaving as they did, and he points out bad behavior. Subtly he teaches the audience not to accept everything they see, but to question what is and is not good. Learning to question values that are presented to us in light of God's values is a healthy step in learning discernment. Taking the time to be with our children and to help them begin to evaluate what they see and hear will begin to cultivate their own powers of discernment.

Finally, in an attempt to avoid the pitfalls of hero worship, it is helpful to have an abundance of role models. When a child or a parent has many people around him whom he admires, it helps avoid the tendency to worship one. Where can we find adequate role models for ourselves and for our children in today's world?

Finding Role Models in Today's World

The family fulfills the earliest need for role models. Christopher did not realize that when Susy tried to wear his clothes, she was showing her admiration of him. Next to the parents, the older siblings will become natural examples to the younger children. We must take care that we communicate to our older children that their influence is a privilege rather than a burden. As we express pride and appreciation in their good qualities, they will be encouraged. The small children will want to copy the older ones.

In addition to their parents, our children need other adult role models. My friend Ann was thirteen when her parents divorced. A compassionate Sunday School teacher took an interest in her and began to spend time with her. This Sunday School teacher expected the best from Ann and believed in her. Ann says that the fact that this adult believed in her helped her through her difficult years of coping with her parents' divorce and becoming a teenager.

When I was young, my parents had a group of close friends with whom we shared many happy times. I always knew that if I ever needed anything, I could go to one of these couples. Their commitment to my parents and their interest in my brothers and sister and me gave me a sense of security.

One of my neighbors is a mother of teens and a committed Christian. I asked Allison whom she might go to outside the family if she had a problem. In mentioning this neighbor, she said, "Mom, she understands teenagers and she's easy to talk to."

I'm so thankful that my daughter has other adults in her life whom I admire. She needs adults other than her parents whom she respects and with whom she feels the freedom to talk. If we spend time with other families, our children will get to know other adults. We must creatively provide opportunities for our young children to get to know our own friends. In turn, we should make a special effort to spend time talking with our friends' children. Take the neighborhood children bike riding. Have several young children over for ice cream. There are many ways to help cultivate adult role models for our children.

Recently we had a visitor from Kenya and one from South Africa to dinner. They told many stories of what God was doing in their countries. As the children joined in the conversation, their faith was enlarged by hearing from adults from another part of the world.

Young people can also become good examples for our children to follow. Children almost always look up to children a little bit older than they are. Carefully chosen babysitters can have a positive impact on our little ones. When I was pregnant with my second child and chasing a two-year-old, I was frequently tired. I found a sweet little eight-year-old girl who would come over and entertain my energetic toddler while I rested. She was kind and loving, and her sweetness was a good example to my child.

This spring my son John, who is thirteen, is involved in a small Bible study led by Dean, a college student. Not only has Dean played basketball with the guys, but he has also taught them how to study the Bible. Just being around Dean has had a positive impact on John.

Our children will naturally look for role models in their special interest areas. Sometimes those most publicized will not be the best ones for them to emulate. It's up to us to help them find good ones.

A biography of an athlete who has a strong faith in Christ will encourage our children who are interested in sports. Exposing our aspiring young musicians to good Christian singers will provide an alternative to current negative music. Having a politician speak about the importance of his faith in Christ will encourage a young person interested in politics.

As the children begin to grow up, it's fun to share role models during a special family time. Recently one of the twins told us about Martin Luther King, Jr., while one of the boys chose Saint Francis of Assisi. We've all enjoyed the series of Value Tales (Grolier Press) which are simple biographies highlighting one person in history whose life exemplifies a good value. In addition, Ethel Barrett's series, Great Heroes of the Bible, has been wonderful to read together.

Continual exposure to different role models will greatly enrich our children. Being around other vibrant Christians will encourage their spiritual life. Church camps offer a good opportunity for our children to be exposed to other committed young people and to learn from someone other than Mom and Dad.

When our children reach the teen years, summer is a valuable time for exposure to other Christians. There's much pressure today for kids to work to earn money. Often this is necessary, but sometimes the money goes for more clothes and more gadgets that could be done without. A valuable week spent working on an inner-city project with other teens will have a greater impact on the child's life. A week at a Christian ranch, on a study program, or serving as a camp counselor will go a long way in developing spiritual maturity in our children.

As parents our role is to be continually thinking "exposure" and helping to bring Christian role models into the lives of our families. Not only do our children need good role models, but as parents we also need examples to encourage us.

For four years we lived across the street from Alfred and Marjory Stanway. Bishop Stanway and his dear wife Marjory had spent twenty-five years as missionaries in Africa. After returning to their native Australia to retire, they felt God calling them to the United States to help begin a new theological seminary. They packed up again and arrived to a new challenge. Over the years we became close friends, and we went to them with many questions. Because they were older and had experienced much, they were examples to us. Because we were in the same profession, they were examples to us. Yet it was their absolute trust in the goodness of God that influenced us the most. Being with them made us want to trust God more.

When we were first married, we used to visit the home of Cliff and Billie Barrows. We marveled at the interaction they had with their five children. The natural faith and joy exhibited by their family was an encouragement to us.

Mothers surrounded by toddlers need encouragement from mothers who are at least one season ahead of them. It's such a relief to be able to call another mother and say, "Did you ever experience this and how did you handle it?"

Women who have finished raising their children can be an encouragement to us and bring some perspective to our situations.

Just as our children need continual exposure to good role models, we too need new exposure. Exposure stimulates growth. Spending time with the poor will help us reevaluate our finances. Watching a film on Mother Theresa will challenge our complacency. Talking with third-world believers will enlarge our faith. Hearing stories of God's faithfulness from a variety of believers will encourage us and help us to become balanced Christians.

As we seek to find good role models for ourselves and our children, we must be reminded that we are all role models ourselves. What does this mean and how do we do it?

Being a Role Model for Others

Panic may set in when we consider the fact that someone is looking to us as an example. My life is not good enough! I don't have all the answers! That's right, none of us does. Being a role model does not mean that we are perfect, nor can we ever expect to be perfect. We are all role models to someone whether we realize it or not. The disciple Peter did not realize what an example he would be to so many of us today. Christopher did not realize that he was an example to his younger sisters. Being a good role model basically involves being available to share our lives and the love of Christ with others.

A father of two teenagers, J. L. himself grew up in an unhappy home. Alcoholism was a problem in his family, and his parents divorced when he was eight. With little adult supervision, he often ran away and lived for weeks at a time with other families in his community. One particular family frequently took him in. The father was a busy physician and the mother had four children. Nevertheless, they made room for J. L. within their family. Occasionally, they even took him along on their vacations and had him over to meals.

In this family he saw love, commitment, and joy. Even as a young teenager, he determined that he would one day have a family like this. This family was a haven to him, and in the process provided the role model of an intact family which he was one day to emulate.

Recently, we had a young college graduate to dinner. As we sat down to eat, both twins begged to sit next to their dad. Our guest looked amazed as she exclaimed, "When I was young, no one wanted to sit next to my dad because he yelled at whoever was closest." Sometimes the simplest things which we take for granted are examples to others.

My children have nineteen first cousins. On Johnny's side of the family our children are the youngest, whereas on my side they are the oldest cousins. The bigger Yates cousins have had such a positive influence on my children. When they were difficult, demanding toddlers, they patiently played with them. As my children have grown up, they have continued to look up to their big cousins. Their cousin Sue, a college graduate, works in our city and her influence as a young Christian woman has been an example to my children.

Now my children are beginning to realize that they are examples to their younger Alexander cousins. In experiencing the love and attention from their older cousins, they realize the importance of caring for their younger cousins. We talk about this privilege and we try to think creatively how we can encourage the younger ones.

It is often necessary to remind our children and ourselves that we are examples whether we realize it or not. In a world of shattered marriages and lonely children, a family that is seeking to follow Christ and growing in love for one another may be the strongest message we can bring to a broken world.

We have a responsibility to share our lives with those around us. Perhaps there's a lonely child whose parents work who would benefit from being in your home after school. A three-year-old in the neighborhood might enjoy playing with your five-year-old. The single parent struggling with a career and raising children will welcome an invitation to bring his family to dinner.

We will not always feel like opening our homes to those around us. However, as we reach out in this way we will receive the great joy that comes from giving. Being role models involves being available and seeking to care for those special people that God has placed in our lives and in the lives of our children.

Our challenge is twofold: to begin to expose our families to the positive influences of good role models, and to be willing to be available ourselves as role models to others. The apostle Paul beautifully captures the essence of role models:

"Having thus a fond affection for you, we were well pleased to impart to you not only the gospel of God but also our own lives, because you had become very dear to us" (1 Thessalonians 2:8).

Focus Questions

Meditate on Luke, Chapter 1, focusing on Elizabeth.

1. What character traits does Elizabeth possess that encourage me?
2. What do I learn about the character of God from this story?
3. What steps should I take this week to help my family benefit from role models?
4. Is there someone that we should share our lives with?

Meditate on Psalm 84 as a personal prayer.

SHAPING A CREATIVE CHRISTIAN HOME

The rich black dirt squished between Johnny's toes as he walked among the rows of tall green corn stalks. The strong, proud plants were fairly bursting with large husks of delicious white corn. My husband smiled with satisfaction as he turned the hose on the last few plants. Dressed merely in an old pair of bermudas, he loved this early morning ritual of tending his small garden plot. The corn was always delicious, and many people were amazed at how well his plants did in this tiny space.

Our house stood next door to the church where Johnny served as one of the ministers of a large, vital congregation. Our summer day camp was in full swing, and small children had already begun to arrive for the morning activities.

Suddenly two familiar big blue eyes peered over the fence.

"Hi, Mr. Yates. How is your corn today?" inquired a small boy about four years of age.

"Well, hello there, my friend," replied Johnny. "The corn is doing real well. It seems to like this rich black dirt."

For several days little Ritchie had stopped by the fence on his way to camp to watch the progress of the corn. Even he was impressed at how tall the stalks rose.

A few weeks later we heard from his mom of Ritchie's creative explanation of the amazing corn.

"Mom," he said with a voice full of confidence, "I know why Mr. Yates's corn is so tall."

"Why, son?" replied his mother.

"Well, you see, Mr. Yates is a minister, and ministers are holy people. He works in his garden barefoot, and all that holiness goes through his toes into the black dirt. That is what makes the corn grow so big!"

Young children are curious. They are receptive. And they believe easily. When our home is full of little people, we have an audience that is readily molded into a growing Christian family. The opportunity is wide open, and yet often we are confused as to how to make our families distinctively Christian. Exactly what is a Christian home anyway?

For one thing, it is not a home where perfect parents live. And it most certainly is not a home where the parents have all the answers. Nor is it a place you would want to visit to observe perfect behavior. The occupants of the home do not pride themselves on being better people than their neighbors. The household does not communicate a serious, staid, religious atmosphere.

Rather, a Christian home is simply one whose members are growing in their relationship with Christ as their personal Savior and Lord. This is a life-long process from which there is no graduation. A Christian home is characterized by forgiveness, love, and joy. Its uniqueness sets it apart from other homes. Here, values and lifestyles are shaped according to the principles set down in God's Word. Communication with God becomes natural, and sharing about God with one another is encouraged.

As parents we have been given the unique privilege and responsibility of teaching our children about Christ and training them in how to live as His followers. Our mandate to do this harks all the way back to Moses. In Deuteronomy 6:5-7, we find his challenge to us:

> You shall love the LORD your God with all your heart and with all your soul and with all your might. And these words, which I am commanding you today, shall be on your heart; and you shall teach them diligently to your sons and shall talk of them when you sit in your house and when you walk by the way and when you lie down and when you rise up.

Throughout the Old Testament, there are many examples of Moses' challenge being carried out. Joshua restated this challenge in his farewell address to the tribes of Israel. After recounting numerous examples of God's faithfulness to His people, Joshua challenged them to choose whom they would serve: the God of their fathers or the false gods of their enemies. Joshua has no trouble deciding for his family as he states, "As for me and my house, we will serve the LORD" (Joshua 24:15).

In reflecting on priorities, we are reminded that our first commitment is to Christ, and our second commitment must be to our families, to nurture them in the faith begun in the family of Abraham and completed by the resurrection of Christ. Throughout Scripture, the challenge has been for the parents to assume the responsibility of passing along their faith to their children.

Today the home is still the primary place of Christian education. Too often teaching Christian values is left to the church or to the private school, yet the home is the greatest source of influence upon our children. We have more time with our children than anyone else, and it is one of the great privileges of life to help mold them into children of faith.

We have a large sandbox in our backyard that all of our children have enjoyed over the years. One of the traditional rites of each spring is the trip to the store to get the new sand for the box. The sand from the previous year has become full of leaves, bugs, and popsicle sticks. The first day we fill the box with the new sand, everyone wants to jump in and play. The sand is fresh. It's not yet tarnished by the rocks and weeds that are soon added. Molding the clean crystals into towers and castles is a delight. The sand is soft, and when water is added, it's easy to shape a lovely creation.

Our young children are like this fine fresh sand. When they are small, they are most easily shaped into children who will grow in their love for God. Building a creative Christian home involves the shaping of our small children by teaching them the naturalness of prayer, the relevancy of Scripture, and the encouragement of fellowship.

The Naturalness of Prayer

At dinner one night, Allison, age eleven, prayed, "Lord, please help the babysitter to be able to handle us." Now that was a big need in our family, and when the children were small, it often took two babysitters to handle them. Christopher, age five, was overheard praying, "Lord, help the babies to learn they can't always have everything they want."

Small children have a refreshing sense of honesty and an un-

usual ease in being natural. Indeed, prayer can be more natural
for them than for their parents. We ought to take advantage of this
youthful naturalness as we begin to teach them to pray. The first
step in teaching our children to pray begins with developing our
own prayer life. We may feel awkward or fearful in our prayers,
and yet God desires for us to be able to talk to Him about anything. We want our children to feel a freedom to talk with us
about anything. How much more does our Heavenly Father desire for us to experience this same freedom in coming to Him. We
need not feel ashamed or unworthy. We go to God in prayer not
because of who we are but because of who He is. When we spend
regular time alone in private prayer each day, praying with our
children will become more natural. Our private prayer time provides opportunity to pray for each of our children and for our
families as a whole.

Praying for Our Children

What, then, are some creative ways that we can begin to pray
for our children?

One of the biggest needs we parents have is to have sensitive
and perceptive antennas. We should have antennas that will be
able correctly to perceive the needs of our children. We should be
able to recognize when something is not what it should be with
one of our children. "Oh, Lord, help me to be perceptive and to
be able to recognize individual needs among my small children.
Give me sharp antennas."

In determining the needs of our children, Johnny and I have
found it helpful to get away once a year usually in late summer to
think through our family's needs and goals for the coming year.
We talk about each child's needs in five areas: social, emotional,
physical, mental, and spiritual. Is this child lonely? Does he need
a close friend? Does another child need to learn discipline in study
habits? Who needs a greater sense of humor or a more thoughtful
nature? Which one ought to develop a reading habit? Perhaps a
middle child needs to feel a greater sense of specialness in our
large family. Does one child need a better understanding of God's
unique calling for him? Does one need more exercise? Should one
have fewer extracurricular activities?

As we think through each child's needs in the five areas, we come up with some tentative goals for the coming year to help meet those needs. For example, my lonely child needs a friend. I begin to pray for her to have a special friend and to pray with her for the new friend God is going to give her this year. My goal would be that during the first week of school I would make an effort to meet her classmates and parents and to invite over a child of her choice. Planning ahead some special activities for the children to do when they arrive will ease the awkwardness of beginning a new friendship and will help them both have a good time. We may have to have several children over, one at a time, before a new friendship is begun.

Discussing each child's development in these five areas has enabled us to develop perceptive antennas. Most important, as we write down our observations of the children, this list of needs becomes our private prayer list for that child for the coming year. In discussing the children, we may notice more needs than we do solutions. This can be depressing unless we remember that we are not in this parenting business alone. There is a powerful, almighty God who is even more concerned about our children than we are. He is our partner in parenting. We must take our children's needs to Him and leave them there. Too often we give a concern to God, then we take it back to worry about it a little more. He desires for us to leave our concerns with Him. He will take care of our children in His time and in His way. We are not super parents equipped to solve all of our children's problems. Rather, we are their custodians. Our job is to nurture our children and to bring their needs to their Heavenly Father for Him to meet.

Having prayed for our children's concerns, we can then be encouraged at the end of the year when we look back at our lists and see the surprising ways in which God has answered. Our own faith will grow when we see God at work in the lives of our children.

Not only do we pray for the needs of our children, but there are also specific qualities we should ask God to build into children's lives. I have several that I pray for regularly. My list looks something like this:

- Ability to make decisions
- Ability to discern good and evil

- Sense of humor and of caring for others
- Ability to be a good communicator and listener
- Ability to fail and to cope with failure
- To be a person of integrity
- Ability to attempt the impossible
- Ability to forgive others and to ask forgiveness
- To have a positive outlook and a desire for excellence
- Ability to laugh at self and have a positive self-image
- To put Christ first in his life
- To be secure in parents' love and be kind to all

In order to avoid a sense of being overwhelmed by prayer concerns, I have a small notebook. In the notebook I have a different page for each day of the week with each family member's name. Each day has a different list of items for the family members for whom I am praying. Mondays I may pray for the different social needs of each child, for their current friends, and even for their possible future mates. Tuesdays I have a different list. Simple organization helps me to avoid being overwhelmed with all the concerns I have.

As we pray for our children, it's reassuring to realize that God intimately knows each of them. He has given us exactly the children we need to help us become the people He wants us to be. Our children are a gift from God. They are also His instruments in our lives to mold us, to shape us, and to help us grow. So often we think it is only we ourselves who do the molding and shaping. In fact, we grow through the children He gives us. We can't raise these kids alone. There is no guarantee they'll turn out right. There is no perfect formula for parenting. But there's power in prayer and there's comfort in knowing that the Creator of the children is guiding us and has His hand on us and on our children. He will show us how to mold these precious gifts into the people He has created them to become and in the process we, too, will grow.

Praying with Our Children

One evening as we knelt to pray, four-year-old John said, "Oh, Lord, please help the president to be a good president and tell him to tell the stores to make their prices lower." Our small children are unusually forthright and honest in their concerns! This is a quality to capitalize on in communicating the naturalness of prayer. Parents need a greater freedom of honesty as well. Sometimes there's a reluctance on the part of parents to pray with their children. This comes in part from a fear that if God doesn't answer, the child's faith will be damaged. It can be harder for parents than for the children.

We need to pray honest prayers and to realize that God always answers out of love. I've found that He answers in three basic ways: "yes," "no," and "wait." Perhaps there is a long silence with the wait. That is hard to take; yet we must remember that God is not hampered by our timetables, and He is not limited to working in ways we can predict. He always does what's best, not necessarily what's fast.

When He answers "no," He answers out of love because He knows what's best for us, just as you'd answer "no" if your three-year-old wanted to play with matches. Or perhaps you'd answer "wait" when your fourteen-year-old wanted to date. Often we don't understand the answers, but we need to remember that God can be trusted, and He always answers out of His love for us. Many times he answers "yes."

It's helpful to teach our children the different ways that God answers our prayers and to instill in them a sense that as they pray, God always answers out of His love for them. As we pray with our children, it is important to encourage honesty. God knows what we are thinking and feeling already, so we may as well be honest with Him.

It's all right for a child to say he hates another child, then to ask God to turn the hate into love. Telling God that we are frustrated or mad and asking His help is honesty in prayer. Our children need to capture the sense that Jesus is their best friend and that they can talk to Him about anything. He will understand. Honesty encourages a natural relationship.

Being able to say we don't know is another way to encourage honesty in prayer. There will be times when we do not have the answer to a sticky problem or the wisdom to make a decision. It's helpful, when appropriate, to let our children know this, then together seek God for the answer or solution. Perhaps we don't know if a child will benefit from a gymnastics class. Praying with the small child for God to show the parents what is best illustrates to the child that parents don't have all the answers and that our family's security rests in God. In this way, Christ is seen as the Head of the family rather than mom and dad. In addition, the foundation is laid for a child's ultimate reliance to be on God rather than on his parents.

As we train our children in honest, natural prayer, consider two types of prayer experience: spontaneous and planned. Spontaneous prayers reveal the vitality of the faith. They are prayers that are offered up throughout the day in response to immediate circumstances.

A few weeks ago I was in the pediatrician's office for a checkup for Libby's ears. A small boy was very sick with pneumonia in the room next to us. Doctors were soaking him down and had called an ambulance to take him to the hospital. Libby and I were both sad and concerned for the little boy, so we prayed. Libby prayed for God to heal him and to comfort his mom. It's wonderful to have a place to take our immediate concerns.

Our son came into the house recently totally frustrated over a relationship with another boy. This boy was a bit older and was going through a stage where he continually put down my son. We talked about the problem and my son's feelings. Then we prayed for the other boy to come through this difficult time soon, and for my son to be able to love and not to lower his own standards of behavior. Taking real-life issues to God as they occur is spontaneous prayer. Too often our tendency is to plan to pray later, then we forget. God desires that we bring our concerns immediately to Him.

Just the other day I had an appointment that I was nervous about. My twins were with me, and I shared that I was nervous and asked them if they would pray while I had the appointment. Susy replied, "No, Mommy, I think I should pray for you right now." She reminded her mother of the benefit of spontaneous prayer.

In addition to giving God our immediate concerns, we ought not to forget the power of natural, spontaneous thanksgiving. It's easy to take for granted God's goodness or to forget to thank Him for an answered prayer. "Thank you, Lord, for my new friend who just called to invite me to her birthday party. Thank you, Lord, that you are always my friend even when I feel lonely."

Spontaneous thanks turn our eyes back to our Lord and help us live lives of appreciation.

On the other hand, planned prayer experiences offer us the opportunity to have a regular time of communicating with God. Daily quiet times are an example of a planned time to pray. The most common planned prayer experiences with our children will most likely be at bedtime. It is easy to fall into rote prayers that are the same night after night. As a child, I remember praying repeatedly, "Lord, bless Mom and Dad and the boys and sister Fran and help all the sick people and make me a better person. Amen."

Needless to say, my faith did not grow a great deal. It's helpful to have prayers that enable us to see God answer in the short range, the medium range, and the long range. "Lord, help me get good sleep and not wet my bed tonight" was a common short-range prayer often heard in our house.

"Lord, help Daddy find a good youth minister" was a medium-range prayer that would possibly be answered in the near future.

"Lord, help Sally and her family to come to know you" would be a long-range prayer that we may or may not see answered in our lifetime.

Using the ACTS formula with our children also brings a diversity to their bedtime prayers.[1] Small children love acronyms and in their uninhibited nature, they will teach us the naturalness of prayer as we listen to them talk to God.

Breakfast time can be a wonderful time for each family member to share what they will be doing that day. In a prayer time at the end of breakfast, each person can pray for one another's day. This allows the evening meal to become a sharing of how God answered those prayers.

We have a bulletin board by our kitchen table with pictures of out-of-town friends on it. Each day one family member gets to choose a picture to pray for at the breakfast table. During the Christmas season, we share a Christmas letter we have received at the evening meal, and one child prays for that family.

From time to time we have kept a prayer notebook beside the table. In it we record special things we are praying for and the date we begin. When God answers, we record His answer and the date. We've found this particularly helpful when we are about to move. As we list all the details and concerns involved in a move, we are encouraged later as we are able to look back and see how God answered our prayers. Even for tiny children who do not understand, this record will one day be a memento of God's faithfulness to the family.

Planned prayer and spontaneous prayer both offer the opportunity for the family members to know and to support one another. Parents need to share their personal concerns with their children and ask for prayers. And children should be praying for each other. Nothing builds closeness better than praying together.

How well I remember going to Allison when she was eight and the other children were one, one, three, and five, and saying, "Allison, will you please pray for Mommy. It's five o'clock. I'm so tired and the kids are so cross. Please pray that I won't be a bad mommy during the next couple of hours!" She prayed for me and encouraged me.

Recently, I overheard my two boys praying together over a problem the younger one had. I had encouraged the older one to talk to and pray with his brother. It was natural for him to do this because we had prayed together since they were both quite small.

What do you do when a small child doesn't want to pray? Relax. Sometimes we don't want to, either. However, the child must be quiet and respectful while we pray. This is politeness to God. As we are enthusiastic and persistent in our own prayer life, the small child will eventually want to join in. We want to communicate that prayer is the special joy of talking to our Heavenly Father, not something the small child must do to be a good boy. If there are several children in the family, the reserved one will soon want to copy the others in prayer. Always ask the quiet one what special thing he would like for you to pray for. Don't force. Instead, give God time to bring this reticent child into a relationship with Himself.

If we begin to pray with our tiny infants, prayer will be natural to them as they begin to grow up. Like fresh sand is easily molded, they too will be able to be shaped to enjoy talking with God even before they understand who He is. Then, as they come to know Him whom they have been taught to love, their communication with Him will be natural.

Relevancy of Scripture

Little John came up to his dad recently and said, "Daddy, which do you like to read more—the Bible or Louis L'Amour?"

This was a tough question for my "cowboy" husband. In all honesty, I'm sure he would have to admit that he found Louis L'Amour books more entertaining, but the Bible had a greater impact on his life.

Thankfully, God has not called us to follow Him, then left it up to us to figure out how to do it. He has not placed us in a world of conflicting values and expected us to guess His. Instead, He has given us His Word to be "a lamp to my feet, / And a light to my path" (Psalm 119:105).

Most of us want to follow Christ, and we desire to help our children love Him. We may find ourselves in a position of longing for a strong faith and yet not knowing how to acquire one. There was once a godly man who prayed for many years for his faith to grow. For a long time he did not see any growth in his faith. One day he opened his Bible and read, "Faith comes from hearing, and hearing by the word of Christ" (Romans 10:17). He began to study his Bible, and his faith began to grow.

Peter encourages his friends to be "like newborn babes, long for the pure milk of the word, that by it you may grow in respect to salvation" (1 Peter 2:2).

If we desire to grow in our own faith and to help our children acquire a firm faith, knowing and utilizing God's Word in our lives is essential. In a world of shifting cultural values, there is one authority that stands the test of time: God's Word. As we grow in our own respect for His Word, we will find ourselves naturally imparting to our children a respect for it as the ultimate authority in their lives.

Enjoying Scripture Myself

Just as Deuteronomy 6:5-7 challenged us, we must first have God's Words on our hearts and second, teach them continuously to our children. Perhaps our experience with the Bible has produced boredom and frustration. We are convinced that it is vital, yet we ourselves have rarely experienced its relevancy in our own lives. Hence we feel inadequate in training our children. How can the Word of God become relevant to us as parents?

Although I grew up in a strong Christian home and believed in the importance of the Bible, I did not experience its relevance in my own life until I met Ricky. A strikingly handsome college basketball player, Ricky seemed to have everything going for him. He was interesting to talk to and fun to be with. As I got to know him, I became aware of a depth to his personality that I could not explain. He had a deep assurance about his faith and an amazing ability to be able to relate it to ordinary, everyday situations. He was excited about God's Word.

I had tried many times to read the Bible. Beginning in Genesis, I would do fine until I got to the fourth chapter and the lists of names began. My yawns would become more frequent and my attention span less. Honestly, there did not seem to be much there that related to me. Once again I would put the Bible aside until the next time that I found myself in the right mood.

Ricky, however, had a different attitude about God's Word. For him it was alive and exciting. It was not outdated and it spoke to him. I was curious and frankly wondered if we were reading the same book. I shared my own frustrations with Ricky, and he began to teach me how he studied the Bible. We began in the Gospel of Luke, and as we studied we took a section of the passage writing out several verses as they appeared. Next we wrote down observations about the verses, using the questions "how?", "what?", "when?", "where?", and "why?" to stimulate our thinking. Finally, as we reflected on the observations, we considered the application. Was there anything there that applied to my life right now or that might in the future? We listed any personal applications that came to mind.

At first I felt awkward with this method of Bible study. But as I persisted over a period of time, I grew in confidence and began to see God speaking clearly to me through His Word. Slowly, the Scriptures became relevant to my everyday life.

Just as Ricky was an example and encouragement to me in seeing the relevancy of Scripture, there may be someone who will be able to encourage you. Finding a friend who seems to be enthusiastic about God's Word and asking them to show you how they study will be a motivation and help.

In addition, there are many Bible study guides available on the market today that will aid in enabling us to discover the relevancy of Scripture. Two tools will be helpful to us as we grow in experiencing the relevancy of Scripture in our lives and as we teach our children to value God's Word: focusing on God's promises and thinking through application. One morning after a sleepless night with two crabby babies, I faced a three-year-old who seemed to bump himself and cry every twelve minutes, a five-year-old who was wrongly accused by his parents of breaking a picture (which crashed during the night of its own accord) and dissolved into tears, a dog who tracked mud into the new kitchen, and an eight-year-old who gave everyone orders. Looking into the mirror, I saw a mother who felt like a failure.

I read Psalm 31 and was tremendously encouraged by the promises of God and its specific application to my life:

> How great is Thy goodness,
> Which Thou hast stored up for those who fear Thee
> Which Thou has wrought for those
>   who take refuge in Thee,
> Before the sons of men!
> Thou dost hide them in the secret place of
> Thy presence from the conspiracies of man;
> Thou dost keep them secretly in a shelter
> from the strife of tongues.
> Blessed be the LORD,
> For He has made marvelous His lovingkindness to
>   me
> in a besieged city (Psalm 31:19-21).

Then I began to pray: "God, I'm glad Your goodness is what is important. Today I have been dwelling on my failures. Thanks for reminding me that my focus should be on Your goodness rather than my inadequacies. And Lord, I'm glad You have a lot of goodness stored up for me because I don't, and I need it! Help me remember today to take refuge in You, to picture myself running into Your presence when things get wild, drawing on Your goodness rather than trying to drum up some of my own which just ran out. I'm running to You from these 'five sons of men.' I feel as if these children are in a conspiracy against me. Thank

You for reminding me of Your lovingkindness in my besieged household. Thank You that Your promises are so applicable to my life. God, You must have a twinkle in Your eye as You gaze at me. Thank You for making me laugh as I apply Your word to my life."

Another promise that has been meaningful to me is found in James 1:5: "But if any of you lacks wisdom, let him ask of God, who gives to all men generously and without reproach, and it will be given to him."

Many times I find myself in the position of not knowing how to handle a problem with a child. Perhaps it's the bedtime tantrums or repeated illnesses. What should I do? Whatever the question, I have found it helps to go to God asking for His wisdom that He promised to me in James. He always answers, sometimes not as quickly as I wish but always in His perfect time.

There are thousands of promises for us in Scripture. Taking God up on His promises enables us to see the relevance of His Word in our lives. Unless we act on these promises, we will not benefit from the Word of God. A comparison might be drawn to a neighbor whom you invite to come by some morning for a cup of coffee and a visit. Technically, that coffee belongs to her as you have promised her a cup. However, until she appears at the door to claim that coffee and have a chat, she has not benefited from the promise.

So it is in our relationship with God's Word. Once we begin to take Him up on His promises, we will benefit in experiencing the relevancy of His Word in our own lives. In turn, we will be able to teach our children how to claim His promises and apply them to their lives.

Teaching Our Children the Scriptures

Several young children were discussing what Jesus looked like. "I know," offered one three-year-old with a burst of enthusiasm. "He wears blue jeans, bare feet, a striped shirt and beard and carries a watering can. He waters wilted flowers and people and brings them back to life!"

In teaching our children about God, it is helpful to keep two concepts in mind: certainty and the mystery. Certainty in the faith refers to the certainty of God's love and forgiveness, while mystery involves the how and the why. In the communion service of our church, we say, "We proclaim the mystery of faith. Christ has died, Christ has risen, Christ will come again." Children love a mystery and can accept certainty and mystery at an early age. We live in the certainty that the sun will rise tomorrow, but we also live with the mystery of how this actually began and how it will continue. Children often ask questions about God, and sometimes we will not know the answers. We will continually have questions ourselves for which there seems to be no plausible explanation. While this may be frustrating, in actuality it is a blessing. For if we could understand everything about God, we would remove the mystery, and in so doing lower God to the level of man.

In dealing with our own questions, I've found it helpful to pray, "God, give me an answer to this question or give me a peace about having the question." When answers don't come, I put the question on my imaginary "heaven list." This is a list of all the questions I am going to ask God when I get there. For example, how are predestination and free choice compatible? Why did you give children more energy than mothers? It is okay to have questions.

When we or our children have questions about Scripture, we should look to the many resources available to us to find the answers. When they cannot be satisfactorily answered, we can have the assurance that in God's time He will answer our questions. Usually, we will find that the difficulty in living the Christian life is caused not by what we do not understand but by being obedient to what we do know is true. As we accept the duality of the certainty and the mystery in Scripture, we will be able to move ahead in helping Scripture come alive for our children.

In the same way that we illustrated spontaneous prayer and planned prayer, it is helpful to look at Scripture in these two categories. Using Scripture spontaneously in response to the normal situations that we find ourselves in will teach us the relevancy of God's Word.

Recently my ten-year-old son had a crush on a cute girl on our street. He was in tears as he feared that she did not like him. We talked together about a verse in the Psalms. "Weeping may

last for the night, / But a shout of joy comes in the morning"
(Psalm 30:5). We discussed how Jesus understood just how he
felt, then we prayed and asked God to comfort him and give him
the assurance that joy would come even if right now he was sad.
God did answer; my son did feel better for a while, then he had to
share his feelings again with God and ask again. He's learning to
go to God with his hurt and worries and that God cares and comforts.

Young children are frequently afraid at bedtime. They cannot
seem to fall asleep and imaginary fears run through their minds.
The Apostle Paul wrote, "God has not given us a spirit of timidity, but of power and love and discipline" (2 Timothy 1:7).

In addition, in Philippians, Paul reminds us that we need not
worry about anything. Instead, we should tell God all our worries
and ask for His peace. He then gives us a list of things to think
on. "Whatever is true, whatever is honorable, whatever is right,
what is pure, whatever is lovely and whatever of good repute, if
there is any excellence and if anything worthy of praise, let your
mind dwell on these things" (Philippians 4:8).

In comforting my fearful child, I share these promises with
her. I explain that God has not given us a spirit of timidity. He has
told us that we can tell Him whatever we are worried about, and
He will deal with it and give us His peace instead. We pray together giving fears to God. It is important to replace the worried
thoughts with positive ones, as Paul suggested. In an attempt to
do this, I tell my child to imagine her next birthday party. She
might think about whom she would like to invite and plan what
she would like to do at the party. This enables her to fall asleep
thinking of happy things.

Reacting to situations as they occur with comfort and Scripture will enable our children to experience the power that is available in God's Word. Planned times together in the Word of God
will also help in building a creative Christian home. Small children have a tremendous capacity to memorize. Memorizing
Scripture together will benefit everyone. Discussing how one
might apply the memory verse in their lives will make it much
easier to remember the verse. Perhaps the family might learn one
verse a week together. Reminding one another of the verse at
breakfast, then being aware of opportunities to apply the Scrip-

ture in our lives throughout the day will enable us to experience
the practicality of God's Word.

Music provides another opportunity for a joyful way to learn
Scripture. There are many children's praise tapes available that
set Bible verses to music. In addition, many of the great hymns of
the faith contain tremendous Biblical principles. Automobile trips
are one occasion in which music can be used effectively.

Reading Bible stories to our children from an early age will
familiarize them with wonderful stories and enable them to get to
know God as they observe how He interacts with His children.
Take care to select good Bible story books with lots of pictures.
When children begin to read, they will appreciate having their
very own Bible and a new marker. With this special marker, they
can begin to underline verses that are special to them.

It's fun to read a small section from the Bible during a family
time and let each child mark the verse that means the most to
him. Then have him share it with the rest of the family telling
why he chose that particular verse. Discovering verses by themselves at an early age will give them confidence in God's Word
and a pride that they too can learn from it all by themselves.

Vacations can offer another opportunity for planned time in
God's Word. Recently we went on a backpacking trip on the Ap-
palachian Trail. During the holiday we studied Moses' adven-
tures while wandering in the wilderness as suggested in *Family
Celebrations.*[2] The second day out on the trail, a huge storm blew
in, and we awoke in our tents to find ourselves shivering and
soaked to the skin. While Johnny hitchhiked home to get a car to
rescue us, we huddled together rejoicing that we did not have to
wander for forty years! The challenges that Moses and his friends
faced certainly made ours seem small. Their story provided us
with much-needed humor and perspective.

Creatively taking advantage of spontaneous and planned opportunities to introduce God's Word to our small children instills
in them a hunger to initiate their own personal study as they
reach the teen years. Blessings come in later years when we take
the time in the early years to capitalize on the openness of our
children. When they are young, they are more open to the molding and teaching by their parents than they will be when they
begin adolescence. The freshness and receptivity of small chil-

dren is an invitation to us to teach them now so that they might develop into young men and women who have an appreciation for the practicality of God's Word.

The Encouragement of Fellowship

Thanksgiving was a special time as we gathered together to celebrate with the Thomsen, Viccellio, and Powell families. Twelve children and eight adults squeezed tightly around the table filled with two huge turkeys. There was much laughter and a sense of naturalness among all the ages. This same group had been celebrating Thanksgiving together for several years.

After stuffing ourselves with turkey, we all packed into one room for a family Thanksgiving service that was planned by the two Thomsen boys. Sam and Rob, both college students, led us in singing. Rob gave each person three kernels of corn. He reminded us that three kernels were the total amount of food which some of the early settlers of America had to eat for one whole day. A basket was passed around into which each person placed his three kernels. For each kernel everyone shared something from the past year for which he was thankful.

Libby was thankful that Allison let her sleep with her sometimes and did not get mad when she wet her bed. John was thankful for his new bat. From the youngest to the oldest, all shared three thanksgivings. These older children were role models to my children; the college boys gave me hope for my boys. Different parents spent time talking to one another's children. The fellowship that took place was an encouragement to everyone.

The encouragement of fellowship is a very old principle. The children of Israel experienced fellowship through their extended families. The first believers in Christ experienced fellowship as they met together to encourage one another in their new faith. "They were continually devoting themselves to the apostles' teaching and to fellowship, to the breaking of bread and to prayer. And day by day continuing with one mind in the temple, and breaking bread from house to house, they were taking their meals together with gladness and sincerity of heart, praising God and having favor with all the people. And the Lord was adding to their number day by day those who were being saved" (Acts 2:42, 46-47).

Fellowship could be defined as spending time together with other believers, the result being that the participants are encouraged in their faith. Recognizing the need for fellowship and making time to experience it as individuals and as families will be another positive force in building a creative Christian home. Fellowship is the implementation of the priority of our commitment to a small group of believers. Being involved in a strong church will offer the best opportunity for experiencing the benefits of fellowship.

In addition, as we seek to spend time with our peers and with other groups, our children will learn the value of that too. When my husband was a lonely freshman on a large college campus, he met Larry who was also a first-year student. Both young men were believers and both were experiencing the challenges to their faith that occur in college. They decided to meet regularly for breakfast to encourage each other in their faith. Sometimes they studied Scripture together; often they prayed; frequently they simply talked. A special bond united the two men, a bond which continues twenty-five years later. A fellowship that began between two scared seventeen-year-old boys over breakfast continues and now includes the next generation.

In the summer months we love to spend time at the family farm. Frequently, family friends join us there. In the evenings we have a tradition of curling up on the hill in sleeping bags to watch the stars come out. The small children delight in counting the stars they see. Sometimes we sing, share, and have our prayers under God's canopy. Recently, our friends Bob and Elaine and their children joined us on the hill. Heidi, their daughter, had just returned from a trip to Mexico with her youth group. They had spent two weeks helping to build a church in an impoverished area. We asked her to tell us briefly what she learned during this experience. Her experiences encouraged me as I saw the wonderful adult she was becoming. Her natural openness encouraged the other children to share as well.

Sometimes an older child will be more self-conscious than a younger one. It may be helpful to ask a small child first to share something personal for which they are thankful or for which they would like us to pray. When a young child is vulnerable, it can make it easier for an older one to share personally.

Spending time with other families who are seeking to grow in their prayer life and in their knowledge of Scripture will be an encouragement to all. Having friends with children older than ours and spending time with those whose children are younger are both important. Being with older families encourages us because their children become role models for ours. Also, older parents enable us to have hope as we draw on their perspective and their wisdom.

Spending time with younger families allows our children to revel in the position of being looked up to. It's interesting to see your young three-year-old suddenly have several two-year-olds following him around wanting to copy his every action. His self-worth zooms up a notch as he finds himself in the role of the big kid for once! Being with young families allows us to have the opportunity to encourage them. As parents, it will also remind us of that earlier season, and we will find ourselves rejoicing that we lived through it.

Fellowship not only offers encouragement to believers, but it also acts as a magnet to draw others to Christ. In Acts 2:47, notice that God added to the fellowship those who also believed. John described in 1 John 1 that our joy is made complete when others join our fellowship. In His high priestly prayer in John 17, Jesus asked that the unity experienced by believers would cause others to know and believe in Him.

The fellowship we experience as believers individually or with families is not meant to be exclusive. It is meant to be shared. There will be times when it is important for believers to be together alone, but there should be other opportunities to invite folks to be with us. As they observe the love we have for one another and the love we show them, they too might come to know Jesus as their Messiah. When we invite others into our fellowship, we are in reality implementing the fourth priority—of caring for those around us who do not yet know God.

A young couple was invited on a church retreat by some friends. Throughout the weekend they heard messages on different aspects of the Christian faith. Even more important, folks reached out to them. Different ones wanted them to play tennis and to join their table for dinner. Through this shared fellowship, they experienced love in a new way, and as a result they too came to know Christ. The couple who had invited their friends on the retreat received a great blessing as they saw God at work answering their prayers for their friends.

When our children watch us make time for fellowship with other individuals, they will unconsciously come to value its importance. When they participate in fellowship as young children, they will be more inclined to seek out its encouragement when they are teens. Fellowship is in reality another means of providing good role models for our children.

This is a season to rejoice in the young ages of our children as we build a creative Christian home. Their youth is our greatest asset. Looking into the sandbox filled with this spring's fresh sand, I noticed the children had already left their play for something else. Behind remained evidence of their happy few minutes. A round mountain firmly packed remained in one corner. The center of the box was occupied by a mound that almost resembled a cake. Car tracks wove in among the objects that looked like squashed hills. The new sand had been firmly molded and in most places still had the clean fresh glaze.

In one corner, however, I noticed a few sticks, a crumpled leaf, and even a dirty gum wrapper. Alas, outside objects were already finding their way into my clean sandbox. As we shape our small children in the naturalness of prayer, the relevancy of Scripture and the encouragement of fellowship, we will be taking advantage of the all too brief season of freshness which youth brings.

Focus Questions

Meditate on Psalm 145.

1. What principles do I find here that would be important to consider in building a Christian home?
2. What two ideas does this passage give me to implement with my children this week?
3. Write a brief poem or story that describes something God has done for you recently to share with your children. (See verse 4.)

Meditate on Colossians 1:9-12, making it a prayer for each family member.

TEN

LOOKING AHEAD
TO THE TEEN YEARS
AND BEYOND

Slowly the sun peers above the horizon casting its first rays of brilliance on a sleepy community. It is barely 7 a.m. at the Yateses, and the phone is ringing again for the third time this morning. Brittany wants to ask the twins what they are wearing to school. Susy and Libby, now nine, have already been on the phone with Nora and Tanya coordinating wardrobes.

Allison, at sixteen, is in a panic. She desperately has to wear the blouse that I have just put on. Would I please take it off right now and give it to her? After all, it is the only thing that matches her blue pants.

As I rush to make pancake batter, Libby appears to tell me that she cannot find matching socks. My washing machine eats socks. Sending her to look again, I return to the pancake batter only to realize—had I put in too much of something or left something out? Balls of paste will not do, so out come the cereal boxes that even today still leave somebody dissatisfied.

Eleven-year-old Chris races through the kitchen announcing that there is no way he has time to eat breakfast. He is still working on his campaign speech for school elections, and he hasn't even combed his hair, which takes ten minutes at least. (Who ever said girls take longer to get ready than boys?) At least Chris has recently decided that he will wait until he graduates from high school to marry.

John finally drags himself to the breakfast table still half asleep. At thirteen, he is our newest teen, and with youthful wisdom he tells us that being a teenager means that "you don't have to have an excuse for being in a bad mood." Breakfast is high-lighted by discussions of who needs the car when, how can John finance a new tennis racket, who will take the gymnastics car-pool, when can Susy get her hair cut, and how will Dad be at three different meetings he has scheduled at the same time to-night. "We'd better pray quickly," Allison reminds us, "because it's 7:10 and time to leave for school."

As everyone heads out the front door, Chris turns to me and says, "Boy, Mom, it must be nice to stay home all day and do nothing!"

The scene has changed; the characters are the same. Kids do grow up, then we have teenagers. This new season is full of ex-citement, challenge, and just plain fun. With all the horror stories you hear today of raising adolescents, a deep dread can permeate the emotions of a mother on the brink of having teenagers. In contrast to the gloomy forecast for this season, I've found it to be a tremendous amount of fun.

Not too long ago I hit that often dreaded benchmark—forty years of age. My younger sister called to offer her sympathy as did many other friends, most of whom were younger. "You've got it all wrong," I told my sister. "Forty is wonderful!" Indeed, it was much better than thirty was for me.

At thirty, I thought I was forever pregnant and did not know what it meant to sleep through a night. I wondered what it was like to have a sense of accomplishment and found it difficult to feel rested enough to enjoy the season. At forty, if the kids are older, you sleep through the night; you have more time to finish projects and to exercise. You enjoy your children as friends, and you mar-vel at the uniqueness of each one.

Are the kids perfect? Heavens, no! Have we succeeded in par-enting? No. Does one ever feel she does? It's simply a new season with new challenges and different blessings. Yesterday we were up during the night with babies. Today we are up waiting for them to come home. Yesterday we were physically exhausted by the de-mands of small children. Today, we are emotionally exhausted as we struggle to meet the needs of adolescents. Yesterday the puzzle was figuring out if a child was sick enough to go to the doctor. Today, it's the sixth-grade math book that we don't understand. Yesterday the challenge for the conscientious mother was how to teach a child to read. Today the challenge is to keep fresh and enthusiastic when the youngest child makes it through that worn copy of *Green Eggs and Ham*.

Each season has new challenges, yet as we walk through the different seasons, we discover that the principles remain the same. How we apply the principles changes with the needs of each season, but the basic ingredients that enable a family to grow in Christ are effective in every season.

In what ways can these same principles encourage mothers of older children?

Retain the Principles

As I find myself in a new season, I am reassured when I realize afresh how true and how practical are the basic principles of mothering that we have discussed. When we begin to implement the principles with small children, the years with older children will be ones of greater confidence and encouragement. Mothers with small children have much to look forward to. Here is a glimpse.

Our Self-Worth

The big challenge to our self-worth is during those years with small children. The four agents—frustration, fatigue, guilt, and failure—are not as dominant in the life of a mother of older children.

Frustration lessens because now our children are in school, and we have time to be involved in activities outside the home that bring fulfillment. In addition, we are able to have some free time in our homes to complete projects. Having a sense of accomplishment reduces frustration. There are, however, new causes of frustration that we may experience.

A mother who has poured her life into her children and derived much satisfaction from it may tend to panic when the last one gets on the school bus. Suddenly, she is not needed in the all-consuming way she was. Frustration grows as she wonders how to spend her time.

The "do-er" must avoid the tendency to join everything. Numerous opportunities arise, and a wise person takes some time to consider where to become involved. There is a false sense that busyness leads to fulfillment. Instead, it leads to frustration. On the other hand, the "be-er" may need to be encouraged to become involved in something meaningful, utilizing the talents God has given her. Both should carefully consider what God has planned for them and not rush into many commitments in an attempt to feel worthwhile.

When the twins started school, a wise older friend urged me to take several months off, avoiding any long-term commitments. I needed time to consider what my involvements should be. As this new season begins, frustration lessens when we seek God's plan for our lives by considering the needs of our families and our gifts and interests.

Fatigue decreases as our children grow up, or at least it takes on a different form. Whereas physical exhaustion plagues mothers of toddlers, emotional exhaustion can be a challenge for mothers of adolescents. Their needs are much more complex than those of small children, and thus they are more mentally and emotionally challenging to mom.

A mother of older children must guard against the temptation to deplete all of her emotional-mental energies outside the home in a career or volunteer work. These older children need those energies when they come in from school. We must be sharp for our children and not mentally and emotionally drained.

Guilt takes on a different form for older mothers as well. One example might be in our worry over a particular child because of his birth order. Perhaps we feel guilty because we were too strict with our first child. Or our middle child did not get enough attention. Was I too lax with my youngest? Naturally, we made mistakes, but we must remember that it was God who determined the birth order of these children. God knows our children better than we do, and He put them in the order that was best for them and for our whole family.

We may suffer guilt over some errors we made in parenting that are only now becoming evident in one of our children. Whatever they are, God can redeem them. God is always at work restoring and rebuilding. As we seek His help and the wise counsel of Christian friends, we will be able to see good come out of any situation.

Failure may appear in a different manner as well. One mother may hear another mother talk about how outstanding her children are. Perhaps they are exceptional athletes, student body leaders, or strong academically. To a mother whose children are average or have learning disabilities, the question may arise, What did I do wrong?

Don't ever listen to that question! It is not a valid question. Our children are all different, and in their differences their value will emerge. We do not yet know the outcome. They are His, and our concern is doing the best we can and entrusting them to Him. We will make many mistakes and experience failure as we parent every age. Acknowledging our failure and moving ahead will enable us to grow from our mistakes rather than be overcome by them.

Generally, the teen years provide a big boost for the self-worth of the mother. Frustration, fatigue, guilt, and failure do not now seem to be the strong agents of discouragement they were in the early years. In part, we have learned how to deal with them. We now seek creative solutions to these common challenges. In addition, the nature of this new season brings welcomed relief.

Seasons

The greatest blessings that come in the season of older children are confidence and perspective. We have made it through those busy years of small children. Our confidence has grown as we look back and see that we did do some things right in training our young children. We have acquired some wisdom that comes only through experience. Now new mothers call us for advice!

In retrospect, some of the challenges and problems that seemed so overwhelming were not that crucial after all. We have seen God's faithfulness to us in the season of young children. This makes it easier for us to believe in and to trust in Him to meet our needs in this new season with older kids.

As we enter the season with older children, we must have a spirit of expectancy. God has some special things to teach us in each season, and as we look to Him expecting to learn, we will be blessed. This season is one to treasure, too. Now, in looking back, we do see how quickly our children grow up. This makes us want to savor the years we have with them before they leave home.

Our relationships with our children have begun to change.

They are becoming adults, and we must allow them room to become independent. Listening to our children, asking for their advice, and acting on their ideas will encourage this growth. They will see things that we do not and have ideas better than ours. This should not threaten us but make us grateful.

During the preteen and teen season, we will find much joy in doing things with our children. Our friendships will strengthen when we enjoy common hobbies and interests. Taking family trips and making new discoveries together will strengthen the relationships. It is indeed a season in which we have found that we would rather be with our own children than with anyone else. They are nearly adults and their companionship is precious.

Finally, in this season of older children, we will be able to see the benefits of those early years of training. Those hours of teaching manners were worth it, as we observe our children relating to other adults. We are not yet finished, but most of the training is done, and now we can enjoy the results.

There will be difficult times in our relationships with our teens. Yet, because we experienced God's faithfulness, we know that He will bring us through whatever we face as we continue to trust Him in this season.

Priorities

The greatest blessing of living by the four priorities is the continual evidence that they apply in every season and in any situation. A person who experiences a "peace that passes all understanding" is a person who had learned to live by those Biblical priorities—commitment to Christ, commitment to our family, commitment to the body of Christ, commitment to the work of Christ.

These priorities are relevant for the mother of adolescents as well. However, the implementation of the priorities may be different now that the children are older.

Our first priority, commitment to Christ, may have unique challenges. For example, I have found it more difficult to be regular in my devotional times alone with God. When I was surrounded by small children, I was desperate. Rising early before children or hiding under the hairdryer to pray and study God's Word was absolutely essential for me each day to be able to cope pleasantly with five small people. Now as five big kids leave for school, it is easy to fill that free time with other "important" things, neglecting what is really the most important. The challenge is to remain faithful to spending time alone with God first, knowing that other commitments will fall into place. As Matthew said, "Seek ye first the kingdom of God and His righteousness, and all these things will be added unto you" (Matthew 6:33).

In this season, as we pray for our children, many more of their specific needs will be evident. One child has a test today, another is struggling with peer pressure. Perhaps our relationship with a child is not as healthy as we would like it. We need God's wisdom on the best way to restore it. Our strength and faith still come from studying His Word. Not only does His teaching give us instruction in how to live, it enables us to have confidence and comfort as we live.

As our children begin to have their own personal quiet times, our own lives will be enriched as we watch them grow and as we have them share with us what they are learning.

Our second priority, commitment to our family, takes on a unique challenge during the teen years. Everyone has so many obligations that home can become simply a stopover on the way to somewhere else. In some aspects, America has become the land of "too much opportunity." Numerous extracurricular activities that are available to our children can keep them occupied from morning until night. Clubs, committees, civic responsibilities, and social obligations could cause parents to be gone every evening. The biggest challenge facing parents of older children involves learning how to say "no" to good opportunities to enable relationships within the family to continue to grow.

The peer pressure from parents as well as from children for kids to play every sport and join many clubs can become overwhelming. A family may realize that they are rarely all together for an evening meal. Recently we had planned a special overnight away as a family. By the time we actually left town, Allison had turned down a date, John a party, Christopher an overnight with friends, the twins a birthday party, and Johnny and I two different dinner parties.

With a large family and numerous opportunities, it can become easy to let time together alone as a family disappear. However, when we make a habit during those early years of spending time together, it will be easier to maintain the priority when overwhelmed by the choices offered to growing children and involved adults.

As we consider our third priority, commitment to our friends, we will find that we seem to spend more time together as families with our children. When our children are tiny, we need a break from them, and we long to have time in fellowship with adults without toddlers present. However, as our children grow up, and our calendar gets more crowded, we will not have that same need nor the time to spend away from our kids. Instead, we will discover a rich blessing in doing things with other families. It is a special time for our children to get to know our friends as adults. Often our kids will listen to and seek the advice of our friends. The network of support of several adults whom our children know are their parents' best friends gives them a sense of security. They know there are people other than family who care for them.

For the adults, the passage of time brings a deepening commitment. Having close friends with whom you've laughed, cried, and prayed over many years develops a sense of security and joy. We never outgrow our need for peers to counsel us and to comfort us. When we walk through several seasons together, our friendships will deepen.

Our fourth priority, doing the work of Christ wherever we are, may change somewhat in form as the children grow up. Now we find opportunities to minister together as families. Perhaps we might work together on an inner-city project. Caring for a single-parent family or adopting an elderly couple as "grandparents" will provide families an opportunity to care together.

In addition, we are enabled to become more supportive of each other's involvements. The twins pray for John's Bible study. We encourage Allison as she meets with several girls. The kids pray for their dad's work. Encouraging one another provides a support system whereby we are filled to care for those in need. There is a great sense of mutual sharing as our children become adults. It is no longer that we are giving to our children; instead, now we are able to give to one another and thus to others.

The four priorities are vital in our lives regardless of the season in which we find ourselves. They provide the balance and the guidance for growing in the Christian life.

Marriage

As we look at our marriages during this new season, we will observe many blessings and several challenges.

The biggest benefit will be the fact that we have survived the adjustments of the seasons of newlyweds and small children. If we have worked in overcoming our tendency toward separateness, in acquiring realistic expectations, and in making a priority of spending time together, we will have formed a secure friendship with our mates. If we have faced difficulties in our relationships and worked them out, ours will be a deeper marriage. The patterns established in the early years are crucial because they are the foundation upon which the relationship is built. Our marriages will be characterized by a confidence that seems to say, "With God and each other we can deal with whatever comes." Security will mark our relationship, security that brings a sense of belonging because we know each other so well.

Fun may be a more present element in this season. If we are careful in living by our priorities which involves saying "no" to attractive opportunities, we will find that we are more rested than in the early years. Because we are no longer exhausted, we will be able to enjoy the pure fun of spending time with our mates.

There will be challenges in our marriages during this season as well. The tendency towards separateness never evaporates. It simply takes on new forms which must be recognized. In this season when the wives may have more time, it is important to keep the priority of spending time together at the forefront. There will be the temptation to jump into a career or volunteer activities now that we finally have some freedom. This is important; however, we must take care that we continue to develop our marriages as well. It is too easy to subtly replace children with activity and begin to grow apart in a marriage. Maintaining a regular weekly date will help prevent this tendency. In addition, this season offers the opportunity to begin to develop new interests.

We all have a built-in need to grow in new areas. It may be a new career, a new hobby, or an exciting project. In this season, the wives should begin to reach out and to grow personally in areas which they have had to postpone while the children were at home during the day. Personal growth for both mates is essential. Choosing one new interest that you can do together is important at this time. Working together provides another means for continuing to build a firm friendship.

The caution is that we must never relax in building a strong marriage friendship. In every season we should creatively consider ways in which we can encourage and love each other more.

To my friend Steve, I would say that when we commit ourselves to Christ and to our mates in marriage, we begin a great adventure. In this adventure of being accepted and loved by one person over many years, we catch a tiny glimpse of the love with which God loves us.

Discipline

Discipline is another area in which we will begin to see the benefits of early training. If we have formed a unified strategy and followed through with its implementation when our children were small, it will be evident as they approach adolescence. Our children will have learned that their parents are in control. We mean what we say. "No" means "no" instead of "maybe—if you whine enough." Our expectations have been clear, and the consequences to one's behavior carried out in firm love. This approach has made us trustworthy as parents. Our children know what to expect; thus, they are secure and much less likely to fully rebel. The most exhausting time in discipline should have been the first five years of a child's life, not the teen years. These first years will have determined greatly how the teen years will go.

The visible benefits of learning obedience and self-discipline will become more obvious. Responsibility will be in evidence as our children do their homework and their family chores. Naturally, it will not always be with a happy spirit, but they have learned the lesson of doing things because they are right, not necessarily because they like it.

Self-discipline will be noted as they come in on time from dates or say "no" to riding with a friend who has been drinking. Joy comes for us as we see them seek God's guidance in making decisions.

A positive self-worth will characterize these teens who have learned the value of obedience and self-discipline. Their self-worth will naturally be under attack during these difficult teen years, but a firm, secure background and much encouragement will enable them to come through this trying time.

There will be challenges to our discipline strategy during this season. Yet the principles which we developed with small children remain crucial and applicable during this time. Our first challenge will be to maintain a unified strategy. Many questions will be asked us by our children, and we must agree on what is and is not permitted in a house of teenagers. It's crucial that parents communicate and determine to be united. One parent may be more effective in dealing with older children than the other. This is fine if both parents have discussed their strategy and will stand by each other.

Another challenge for the parent of teens is to discern how much independence to give young adults while maintaining control in needed areas. This is a delicate balance and one of the difficulties of parenting teens. Older children have a greater capacity to argue and to make their case. Sometimes they simply wear out the parents. They will inevitably say, "You don't trust me." That's right; we don't. However, trust is not the best word. We would not "trust" a medical resident to do surgery on us either. He does not have the experience necessary to enable him to do the job properly. Even though our children may be nearly adults, they do not yet have the experience with which to make some wise judgments. Occasionally, they will want control and freedom before they are ready for it. We must remain firm in these times of objection.

Although there are many challenges in training teens, our families will benefit when we implement a discipline strategy based on God's principles with our young children.

Atmosphere

Love, forgiveness, and joy will continue to be three traits which we want to characterize our homes when our children are adolescents. We will enjoy the privilege of seeing our children express these qualities as they become older.

They have begun to learn the value of service, acceptance,

and appreciation. When we first taught them to set the table for the evening meal, they complained. Now we might hear them occasionally ask, "Is there anything I can do to help, Mom?" When they were toddlers just two years apart in age, it seemed they would never get along. Today we overhear them giggling as they curl up together doing Spanish homework. We used to feel we had to remind them constantly of those magic words "please" and "thank you." Today we hear them say, "Thanks for letting me have all my friends over, Mom."

Growing in forgiveness will continue as parents set the example. When we ask our children's forgiveness or our mate's, it will enable the atmosphere to be one where forgiveness is expected. The natural enthusiasm of growing children will bring lively joy to the atmosphere of our households. We may find that we collect neighborhood children if our homes radiate a positive, happy environment.

When our homes become gathering places, we have a challenge unique to this season. Teens and preteens need a place to hang out, and our homes should be open to this opportunity. It will mean the sacrifice of time and energy on the part of the parents, yet it is a need unique to this season and a wonderful way in which we can influence the lives of young people.

Phil and Irene have four children, three of whom are teenagers. Their home has always been the place to "hang out." They are a strong Christian family and have limits for behavior which the teens accept and abide by. Their willingness to be available has had a positive influence on many teenagers. It has taken much of their personal time to be available in this way, yet the blessings have been great. The challenge of an open home will be one parents of teens must face. Another challenge for parents is achieving the balance between reminding and appreciating. If we are always telling them to do their homework, wash their face, fulfill certain responsibilities, we will become nagging moms, and the atmosphere in our homes will become negative. This is a season in which we must begin to pull back and let them assume more personal responsibility. Naturally, they will need to be reminded of things—teens have short memories—yet we must balance these reminders with statements of acceptance and appreciation.

A final challenge is that of maintain... in a household of teens. Often to a teenag... and we may be tempted to overreact. It is ... knowing that tomorrow this "crisis" will ... seems today.

The companionship that older children pr... mendous joy into the atmosphere of the home... develop, their individual talents will become m... ...ent. Encouraging them to use their gifts in the home will bring a delightful uniqueness to the atmosphere.

Love, forgiveness, and joy will continue to be traits we want to encourage with our young adults. As these traits are evident and growing, our homes will become gathering places for all ages and a refuge to a world looking for love.

Role Models

By the time our children leave the toddler years behind, we will have benefited from the wisdom and the experience of many older women who have encouraged us as we coped with small children. In addition, we will have begun to see our children benefit from exposure to good role models.

The value of role models now takes on an even greater importance for our teenagers. As they seek to become independent from us, they need to know other people who exhibit the character traits we have been emphasizing.

During their teen years, our children will be greatly influenced by those attractive teens a few years older than they are. This natural move toward independence provides us with a tremendous chance to expose our children to good role models. The negative parent who simply criticizes friends or older teens is missing out on an opportunity. One way to weed out negative influences in our children's lives is to replace them with positive ones. Consider the child's natural interests and gifts and seek an older teen with similar interests and values you approve of. Exposing our young people to exciting church youth ministries and meaningful summer camps will be ways to utilize older teens as role models.

Encouraging our children to evaluate the media is another step in training them to recognize good role models. Mealtimes

ment opportunity to ask thoughtful questions. What
s a political figure giving? What do you think of what he
ing and why? Television advertisements provide a clear ex-
mple of evaluating truth. What does this ad promise? Do you
think it will really happen?

During these years, other adults become role models to our
children in a new way. One child may be more receptive to hearing the same advice from another adult than she would from us.
This is normal, and it will be more likely to happen if the child
has built up a relationship with the adult during his formative
years. As parents, we will greatly benefit when we take the time to
know and to care for our friends' children.

In addition to the need for providing role models for our children, the challenge remains for us and for our children to be
available as role models. Recently, sixteen-year-old Allison and I
were working on a commercial together. During the filming, we
got to know a teenager named Michelle. Michelle's parents had
divorced when she was four, and as a result she had determined
never to marry. To her it was a no-win situation. As Allison and I
together talked with her, she began to have hope that she could
someday have a wonderful marriage. For me the blessing of this
conversation was not only encouraging Michelle but also listening
to my daughter as she interacted with her.

The value of role models will be important for us and for our
children as we enter each new season. When we learn from another person's wisdom, experience, and objectivity, we will be
uplifted. As we observe their faith, we will be challenged. Our
role as parents is to seek out role models for ourselves and for our
children who will encourage us to walk in the paths that God has
planned for us.

Creative Christian Homes

The naturalness of prayer, the relevancy of Scripture, and the
encouragement of fellowship still remain three essential ingredients in a home with older children.

The form of communicating these principles will change.
Whereas the parents had to assume most of the teaching with
small children, now we find ourselves being taught by our young

adults. Gradually, the focus is shifting to our growing together in our relationships with God.

Because our children are older, their understanding of prayer will be more on the level with ours. Our concerns will be similar. Our sharing will be deeper. They can join with us in great understanding as we pray for an ill friend, a job problem, or a college choice. A greater leadership role should be taken by our children in family prayer times. Rather than our being the ones who lead in prayer, often we should let them take charge. Encouraging our children to pray for and with each other is of continual importance. We might find it helpful with young adults to share the five areas of growth—social, emotional, physical, mental, and spiritual. Have each family member take some time alone to think through his own needs for the coming year in each of these areas. Then have a time in which each person can share some of his own desires in these areas as prayer requests. As our children begin to recognize their own needs and determine their own goals in each area, they are growing in maturity. In praying for each other in this manner, we become partners with each other in Christian growth.

The relevancy of Scripture will become more important in the young adult's life. Providing our children with well-written study guides geared to their level will encourage their own personal quiet times. In family study times, we should also allow them to take more leadership. Perhaps one child could provide the "sermon" during a vacation family worship service. Another child could share a special promise from Scripture during family devotions.

Exposing our children to the many exciting biographies of Godly men and women will encourage their faith. Challenging them to choose projects that will cause them to ask tough questions is beneficial, if permitted, in a school class. This is a season in which we want them to begin to ask hard questions and to dig to find the answers. It is most helpful if they experience this when they are still at home, and we can point them to good resources. Our goal is that they know why they believe what they do and that they have a faith that will withstand critical examination.

The encouragement of fellowship takes on a new importance

with older children. Their peers and older teens will be instrumental in encouraging the growth of their faith. Providing our children with opportunities to be exposed to other teens who are growing in their faith will be important in this season. Seek out fellowship groups in your community. Explore good camp programs. There are numerous possibilities today, and we should take advantage of them. Our children need to hear the same message from someone other than mom and dad.

Prayer, Bible study, and fellowship will always be three important ingredients of a creative Christian home. Discovering ways to implement them will be a challenge and a blessing for us in each season.

When we begin to live by these eight principles, we will discover that after a period of time they will become internalized. Our instinct will begin to be to look at life in light of the priorities and to respond to situations in accordance with the principles. These principles will become second nature to us and provide for us the security and the blessings of knowing who we are and why we live the way we do.

Our homes are each unique. Our children are different, and our needs are constantly changing. In applying these principles, we must remember that God is faithful, He does not change. We can rejoice in Him!

Rejoice in the Lord

Often in our lives as busy mothers, we may find ourselves so focused on our roles that we forget to rejoice in the Lord. As we walk through our daily activities, we will discover that our eyes are usually on one of three places: on ourselves, on our circumstances, or on other people.

When our eyes are on ourselves, we will become disheartened. Our inadequacies may overwhelm us. Perhaps we are unorganized. We may be lousy cooks. Mothering might not come natural for us. Self-pity will become a companion if we concentrate on our weaknesses. Looking at our circumstances may cause us to become complainers. Someone else's situation may appear to be better than ours. A friend with one child may have a large home, whereas we have several children living in a tiny house. A neighbor's child may be outstanding in many areas while ours is average. It may become easy to focus on what we do not have when we dwell on our circumstances.

If we allow our eyes to dwell on other people, we can become frustrated, jealous, or even bitter. Perhaps a friend of ours seems to have everything. Maybe her husband is most attentive to her and helps her with the children. Another mom may be prettier or more talented than we are. Concentrating on other people can cause us to develop a critical attitude.

Obviously, we cannot wear blinders, but God desires that our eyes rest on Him. As we look first to Him, then we will be able to view ourselves, our circumstances, and other people with eyes of appreciation. Whenever we feel discouraged, it is helpful to run an "eye check" and ask on whom are we focusing. Usually, we will find that we are concentrating on one of these three areas, and we must cast our eyes back on the Lord in order to rejoice.

The writer to the Hebrews said, "Therefore, since we have so great a cloud of witnesses surrounding us, let us also lay aside every encumbrance, and the sin which so easily entangles us, and let us run with endurance the race that is set before us, fixing our eyes on Jesus, the author and perfecter of our faith" (Hebrews 12:1-2).

As we practice focusing our eyes on the Lord, we will be reminded that He is good, that His ways are not our ways, and that His timing is not our timing.

God Is Good

How easy it is to forget that God is good. Once when we were trying to find a home, I prayed specifically for a certain one that seemed to be exactly right. I was sure we would get this home. However, our offer was turned down and I was disappointed. Alf Stanway said, "Susan, God has answered your prayer for that house with a 'no.' It is a 'love no.' He knows what your needs are, and He has something better for you. You must trust in His goodness." He was exactly right.

God's goodness and His love for us are not based on our goodness. His love is not determined by how we perform in raising our children. His love does not depend on our being good wives. He loves us and wants the very best for us simply because we are His.

As Isaiah said, "But now, thus says the Lord, your Creator, O

Jacob, and He who formed you, O Israel, do not fear, for I have redeemed you; I have called you by name, you are Mine" (Isaiah 43:1). We belong to God. God's love is a spontaneous love. It is not caused by our worth, but by our need. The plans God has for us are good. He wants us to know His will, and He equips us to do it. As Psalm 32:8 states, "I will instruct you and teach you in the way which you should go; I will counsel you with My eye upon you."

As we attempt to raise our children according to Biblical principles, we can have the confidence that God is good. His love for us never changes. His plans for us are the best.

His Ways Are Not My Ways

In Isaiah 55:8 we read, "My thoughts are not your thoughts, neither are your ways my ways, declares the Lord."

What a wonderful statement this is. Often we expect God to work in something the way we would, and yet we forget that He is far more creative than we are. He alone knows the future. He is not limited by our experience and human knowledge. Instead, He is the author of all knowledge.

His ways will sometimes confound us. His methods might be unique. For example, how unusual to send the King of kings, His own Son to be born in a lowly cave to a simple, unwed mother. Instead of being treated as royalty, He lived a brief life of service and suffered a humiliating, painful death deserted by His closest friends.

To change the world He chose twelve men who were not especially outstanding. He spent only three years training them, and during His last days they still did not fully understand His purpose.

As we see Biblical examples of God's ways, we can be encouraged that He is indeed working in our families. He has given us exactly the children that we need to enable us to become the women He desires for us to be.

Johnny and I always wanted four children. We prayed many years for four healthy children. When our fourth turned out to be five, we were amazed. God knew that we needed these twins to help mold us into the people He desired for us to become. He has used these two in my life as agents of growth in so many ways. His plan has been far better than mine.

When things happen in each of our lives that we do not understand, we need not fear. We must remember that God is still in control. We may not understand His ways at the time, but we can have confidence that they are the best. Ultimately, God's purposes will be revealed. As we look back over our lives, we will see His faithfulness to us.

His Time Is Not My Time

Isaiah tells us that "Those who wait for the Lord will gain new strength; they will mount up with wings like eagles, they will run and not get tired, they will walk and not become weary" (Isaiah 40:31).

As we grow in our faith, we will often feel like we are waiting on God to answer a prayer, or change a situation, or help a child. Much frustration results simply because we have to wait. We live in an instant generation. We are always in a hurry. We hurry to grow up. Then we hurry our children. I've often thought that when I come to the end of my life and look back, what I will regret the most is that I hurried through it.

A restaurant in our town has a timer for each table. When the waitress takes an order, she begins the timer. If she has not returned with the food in fifteen minutes, the meal is free. The presumption is that clients are in a hurry. In New York City, there is another restaurant where a timer is set for one hour per table. At the end of your hour, you are asked to leave in order that others may take your table. The owners are in a hurry to fill tables and increase profits.

We must recognize our tendency to demand instant answers and to hurry to achieve. We live in a world of time-oriented creatures. God, however, is not bound by our timetables. He is not in a hurry. He is interested in the process as much as in the product. This is why He often answers our prayers with a "wait." He has an eternity to develop us. God always does what is best, not necessarily what is fast.

Ingrid Trobisch has often said that a Christian is one who has learned to wait. This is a difficult lesson as we are by nature impatient people. However, as we focus on God, we can be reminded that His ways and His timing are the very best for us. In waiting, we will learn valuable lessons if we keep our eyes on Him.

In retaining the principles of parenting and rejoicing in the Lord, we will be encouraged as we seek to be the mothers God has created us to be. His desire is that we cherish this privilege and enjoy the season that we are in right now.

As we turn our eyes on Him, we will be reminded that

- HIS MERCY IS EVERLASTING: He will forgive us still another time when we fail to trust Him with our circumstances, and worry instead.
- HIS UNDERSTANDING IS PERFECT: He knows how it feels to be frustrated, tired, or overwhelmed.
- HIS LOVE NEVER ENDS: We cannot cancel it or improve upon it. His love for us is the most it can ever be.
- HIS POWER IS COMPLETE: There is nothing too insignificant or too difficult for Him to handle.
- HIS CHARACTER IS ALWAYS FAITHFUL: He never leaves us or gives up on us.

Now to Him who is able to do exceeding abundantly beyond all that we ask or think, according to the power that works within us, to Him be the glory in the church and in Christ Jesus to all generations forever and ever. Amen (Ephesians 3:20-21).

Focus Questions

Meditate on Psalm 103.

1. Describe the character of God from these passages.
2. What are some specific promises He has for me there?
3. How can I benefit from this psalm in my life today? this week?

Meditate on Psalm 105.

This is an example of the children of Israel remembering God's faithfulness to them. Write your own psalm of thanksgiving to God, being specific about the many ways He has been faithful to you.

END NOTES

Chapter 4: Establishing Priorities That Work

1. Corrie Ten Boom, *Don't Wrestle, Just Nestle* (Old Tappan, N.J.: Fleming H. Revell Co., 1978).
2. James C. Dobson, Focus on the Family, 801 Corporate Center Drive, Pomona, CA 91768.
3. Howard Hendricks, *Heaven Help the Home* (Wheaton, IL.: Victor Books, 1974), p. 22.
4. John DeFrain and Nick Stinnet, *Secrets of Strong Families* (New York: Berkley Books, 1985), p. 14.
5. John Yates, *For the Life of the Family* (Wilton, Conn.: Morehouse-Barlow, 1986).

Chapter 5: Becoming a Best Friend in Marriage

1. David Fenell, as quoted in Sally Squires, "Long-Married Couples Explain How They Stay Together," *The Washington Post*, November 10, 1987.

Chapter 9: Shaping a Creative Christian Home

1. See page 58.
2. See Ann Hibbard, *Family Celebrations* (Brentwood, Tenn.: Wolgemuth & Hyatt, Publishers, 1988).